Foundation

Pearson Edexcel GCSE (9-1)
History

Crime and punishment through time, c1000–present

Series Editor: Angela Leonard
Authors: Darryl Tomlin Victoria Payne Dan Hartley Trevor Sharkey

Pearson

Published by Pearson Education Limited, 80 Strand, London, WC2R 0RL.

www.pearsonschoolsandfecolleges.co.uk

Copies of official specifications for all Pearson qualifications may be found on the website: qualifications.pearson.com

Text © Pearson Education Limited 2020

Series editor: Angela Leonard
Produced by Florence Production Ltd, Devon, UK
Typeset by Florence Production Ltd, Devon, UK
Original illustrations © Pearson Education Limited
Illustrated by KJA Artists Illustration Agency and Phoenix Photosetting, Chatham, Kent, and Florence Production Ltd, Devon.

Picture research by Integra
Cover photo © Science Photo Library / Sheila Terry

The right of Darryl Tomlin, Victoria Payne, Dan Hartley and Trevor Sharkey to be identified as authors of this work has been asserted by her in accordance with the Copyright, Designs and Patents Act 1988.

First published 2020

23 22 21 20
10 9 8 7 6 5 4 3 2 1

British Library Cataloguing in Publication Data
A catalogue record for this book is available from the British Library.
ISBN 978 1 292 35013 4

Printed in Slovakia by Neografia

A note from the publisher
1. While the publishers have made every attempt to ensure that advice on the qualifications and assessment is accurate, the official specification and associated guidance materials are the only authoritative source of information and should always be referred to for definitive guidance. Pearson examiners have not contributed to any sections in this resource relevant to examination papers for which they have responsibility.

2. Pearson has robust editorial processes, including answer and fact checks, to ensure the accuracy of the content in this publication, and every effort is made to ensure this publication is free of errors. We are, however, only human, and occasionally errors do occur. Pearson is not liable for any misunderstandings that arise as a result of errors in this publication, but it is our priority to ensure that the content is accurate. If you spot an error, please do contact us at resourcescorrections@pearson.com so we can make sure it is corrected.

Websites
Pearson Education Limited is not responsible for the content of any external internet sites. It is essential for tutors to preview each website before using it in class so as to ensure that the URL is still accurate, relevant and appropriate. We suggest that tutors bookmark useful websites and consider enabling students to access them through the school/college intranet.

MIX
From responsible sources
FSC www.fsc.org FSC™ C128612

Contents

How to use this book

What's covered?

This book covers the Thematic study on Crime and punishment through time, c1000 to present. These units make up 30% of your GCSE course, and will be examined in Paper 1.

Thematic studies cover a long period of history, and require you to know about change and continuity across different ages and aspects of society. You will need to know about key people, events and developments and make comparisons between the different periods studied.

Linked to the thematic study is a historic environment that examines a specific site and its relationship to historical events and developments.

Features

As well as a clear, detailed explanation of the key knowledge you will need, you will also find a number of features in the book:

Key terms

Where you see a word followed by an asterisk, like this: Treason*, you will be able to find a Key Terms box on that page that explains what the word means.

> **Key term**
>
> **Treason***
>
> Betraying the king – for example, by helping his enemies, or plotting to kill or replace him.

Activities

Every few pages, you'll find a box containing some activities designed to help check and embed knowledge and get you to really think about what you've studied. The activities start simple, but might get more challenging as you work through them.

Summaries and Checkpoints

At the end of each chunk of learning, the main points are summarised in a series of bullet points – great for embedding the core knowledge, and handy for revision.

Checkpoints help you to check and reflect on your learning. The Strengthen section helps you to consolidate knowledge and understanding, and check that you've grasped the basic ideas and skills.

The Challenge questions push you to go beyond just understanding the information, and into evaluation and analysis of what you've studied.

Sources and Interpretations

This book contains numerous contemporary pictorial and text sources that show what people from the period, said, thought or created. You will need to be comfortable examining sources to answer questions in your Paper 1 exam.

Although interpretations do not appear in Paper 1, the book also includes extracts from the work of historians, showing how experts have interpreted the events you've been studying.

> **Source A**
>
> An engraving showing the execution of Guy Fawkes and his fellow conspirators, produced in 1606.

> **Interpretation 2**
>
> From *Victorian England, Portrait of an Age* by G.M. Young, published in 1936.
>
> His frigid efficiency covered an almost passionate concern for the welfare of the people.

Extend your knowledge

These features contain useful additional information that adds depth to your knowledge, and to your answers. The information is closely related to the key issues in the unit, and questions are sometimes included, helping you to link the new details to the main content.

> **Extend your knowledge**
>
> **The Tyburn tree**
>
> The most famous area where public executions took place was at Tyburn (now Marble Arch) in London. The Tyburn tree ultimately developed into a man-made gibbet (scaffold) large enough to hang 24 people at once, on what were known as 'hanging days'. These days attracted crowds of thousands.

Exam-style questions and tips

The book also includes extra exam-style questions you can use to practise. These appear in the chapters and are accompanied by a tip to help you get started on an answer.

Recap pages

At the end of each chapter, you'll find a page designed to help you to consolidate and reflect on the chapter as a whole. Each recap page includes a recall quiz, ideal for quickly checking your knowledge or for revision. Recap pages also include activities designed to help you summarise and analyse what you've learned, and also reflect on how each chapter links to other parts of the unit.

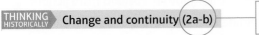

These activities are designed to help you develop a better understanding of how history is constructed, and are focused on the key areas of Evidence, Interpretations, Cause & Consequence and Change & Continuity. In the Thematic Study, you will come across activities on both Cause and Change, and in the Historical Environment on Evidence, as these are key areas of focus for these units.

The Thinking Historically approach has been developed in conjunction with Dr Arthur Chapman and the Institute of Education, UCL. It is based on research into the misconceptions that can hold students back in history.

| THINKING HISTORICALLY | Change and continuity (2a-b) | conceptual map reference |

The Thinking Historically conceptual map can be found at: www.pearsonschools.co.uk/thinkinghistoricallygcse

At the end of most chapters is a spread dedicated to helping you improve your writing skills. These include simple techniques you can use in your writing to make your answers clearer, more precise and better focused on the question you're answering.

The Writing Historically approach is based on the *Grammar for Writing* teaching method developed by a team at the University of Exeter and popular in many English departments. Each spread uses examples from the preceding chapter, so it's relevant to what you've just been studying.

Preparing for your exams

At the back of the book, you'll find a special section dedicated to explaining and exemplifying the new Edexcel GCSE History exams. Advice on the demands of this paper, written by Angela Leonard, helps you prepare for and approach the exam with confidence. Each question type is explained through annotated sample answers at two levels, showing clearly how answers can be improved.

Pearson Progression Scale: This icon indicates the Step that a sample answer has been graded at on the Pearson Progression Scale.

About change

This course is about two things: it is about the history of crime, and it is about **change**. You are going to look at a long period of time – over 750 years. Crime and punishment is the theme you will follow through these years. Concentrating on just one part of British life means you can also focus on how and why things change (and sometimes how and why they don't).

This introduction is to help you understand the language and concepts historians use when they discuss change.

- **Change** – this is when things become different than they were before.
- **Continuity** – this is the opposite of change, when things stay the same, sometimes for a very long time.
- Change isn't always the same as **progress** – which is when things get better.
- The **rate of change** – change doesn't always happen at the same pace – sometimes things change very quickly, but sometimes they change slowly. Historians are interested in why this is.
- A **trend** is when there are a number of similar and related changes, continuing in the same direction, over a period of time – for example, the fact that there were 57 million people with smartphones in the UK in 2019 is part of the trend in the growing use of mobile phones.

- A **turning point** is when a significant change happens – something that is different from what has happened before and which will affect the future. For example, it was a turning point when Michael Harrison made the first ever mobile phone call in Britain on 1 January 1985.
- Historians are very interested in the **factors** that affect change. Some of them can be quite obvious, but others are more surprising. For example:
  - developments in science and technology, particularly around miniaturisation, have affected the development of the mobile phone
  - people's attitudes have also affected the development of the mobile phone. For example, text messaging (SMS) was not originally designed to be used – it was built in to help scientists test the first networks and phones. But users found out about it, liked it, and it has now become part of our world
  - less surprisingly, government has affected the development of mobile phones – with regulations about networks, laws about using them, and planning control of phone masts.

Look out for plenty more factors that affect change throughout the course.

Activities

1. Write your own definitions for each of the words in bold above, and explain your own example of each one.

2. Graphs can be a useful way to show change. Study the graph opposite.
   a. Where would you put these two factors affecting change on the graph? i) Worries about the health effects of butter are common. ii) Government campaigns to get people to reduce the fat in their diet.
   b. At the same time, bread sales fell by about 50%. Is this a factor affecting spread sales?

3. Study the table summarising Katy and Mel's journeys to school.
   a. Draw a line graph, with two lines, showing Katy and Mel's independence in their journeys. On the x-axis have the school years from 1 to 11. On the y-axis, plot their independence. For each of them, score their two journeys (to and from school) and add the scores together. Going with a parent: scores 1 mark; using public transport: 2 marks; going by themselves: 3 marks. (Use half marks when they sometimes do one thing, and sometimes another: e.g. in Year 8 Katy scores 1½ for her journey to school, because she sometimes goes by car and sometimes goes by bus.)
   b. Explain which period of time on the graph is the best example of continuity.
   c. Does the rate of change vary? Explain your answer.
   d. Is there a trend? If so, explain what it is.
   e. Is there a turning point for either of them? If so, explain what it is.
   f. Explain what factors you think affected the changes in their journeys to and from school.

4. Make a timeline or a graph to show change in your life over time. Show any trends or turning points, and places where the rate of change increases. Explain what factors have influenced these changes.

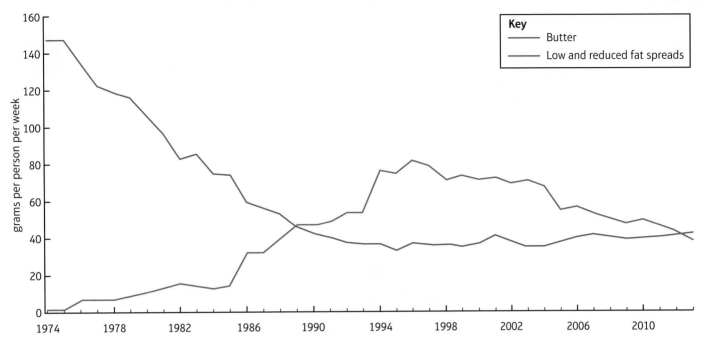

UK purchases of butter and spreads, 1974–2013

Journeys to and from school

School year	Katy	Mel
Years 1–6	Mel and Katy are twins; they went to a primary school that was about 10 minutes walk from home. Their Dad walked with them to school in the morning, and their Mum met them and walked home with them at the end of the day.	
Year 7	They moved to a secondary school which was about three miles away. Their Mum took them to school in the car in the morning. They went to an after school club, and then their Dad picked them up in the car at about 5 o'clock.	
Year 8	Going to school, usually got a lift from her Mum in the car, but sometimes caught the bus with Mel and her friends. Stayed at the after school club until Dad picked them up in the car.	Caught the bus to school with her friends. Stayed at the after school club until Dad picked them up in the car.
Year 9	Cycled to school with her mates Aarav and Claire. Often stayed to do sport after school, and then cycled home.	Caught the bus to school with her friends. Usually stayed at the after school club until her Dad picked her up in the car. In the summer sometimes went home on the bus with her friends.
Year 10	Cycled to school with her mates. Often stayed to do sport after school, and then cycled home. In the summer developed a crush on one of Mel's friends, Callum, and started going in on the bus with Mel and her friends.	Caught the bus to school with her friends. Went home on the bus with her friends.
Year 11	Started going out with Callum. Usually met him on the bus in the mornings, and walked home with him after school.	Caught the bus to school with her friends. Went home on the bus with her friends.

Timeline: Crime and punishment, c1000–present

Anglo-Saxon	Norman	Late Middle Ages	Tudor	Stuart

Crime and definitions of crime

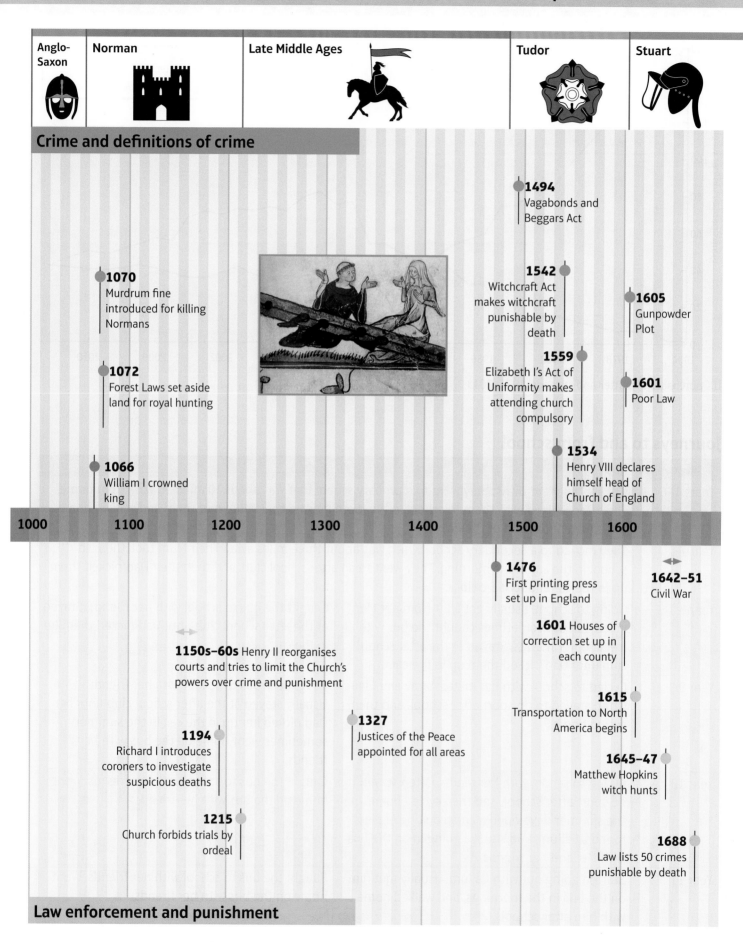

1494
Vagabonds and Beggars Act

1070
Murdrum fine introduced for killing Normans

1542
Witchcraft Act makes witchcraft punishable by death

1605
Gunpowder Plot

1559
Elizabeth I's Act of Uniformity makes attending church compulsory

1072
Forest Laws set aside land for royal hunting

1601
Poor Law

1534
Henry VIII declares himself head of Church of England

1066
William I crowned king

1000	1100	1200	1300	1400	1500	1600

1476
First printing press set up in England

1642–51
Civil War

1150s–60s Henry II reorganises courts and tries to limit the Church's powers over crime and punishment

1601 Houses of correction set up in each county

1615
Transportation to North America begins

1327
Justices of the Peace appointed for all areas

1194
Richard I introduces coroners to investigate suspicious deaths

1645–47
Matthew Hopkins witch hunts

1215
Church forbids trials by ordeal

1688
Law lists 50 crimes punishable by death

Law enforcement and punishment

Georgian		Victorian	Edwardian	World Wars	Modern Era

1723
Black Acts make poaching game punishable by death

1888
Jack the Ripper murders

1976
Domestic Violence Act makes domestic violence a crime

1735
Witchcraft Act defines witches as confidence tricksters

1833
Tolpuddle martyrs

1967
Sexual Offences Act decriminalises homosexuality

1831
Last reported case of highway robbery

1916
Military Service Act introduces conscription

2006
Racial and Religious Hatred Act makes racial abuse a crime

1837
Victoria crowned queen

1939–45
Second World War

1700   1800   1900   2000

1914–18
First World War

1685–1815 Enlightenment – new emphasis on science and reason

1813 Elizabeth Fry begins visiting prisoners at Newgate

1900
Borstals introduced for young offenders

1748
Fielding brothers set up Bow Street Runners

1829
Robert Peel sets up Metropolitan Police

1933
Execution of under-18s ends

1777
John Howard's 'The State of Prisons' published

1832
Punishment of Death Act reduces number of crimes punishable by death to 60

1953
Execution of Derek Bentley

1778
Transportation to Australia begins

1877 All prisons brought under government authority

1842
Pentonville Prison opens

1965
Death penalty abolished for most crimes

1810
Law lists 222 crimes punishable by death

1857
Transportation abolished

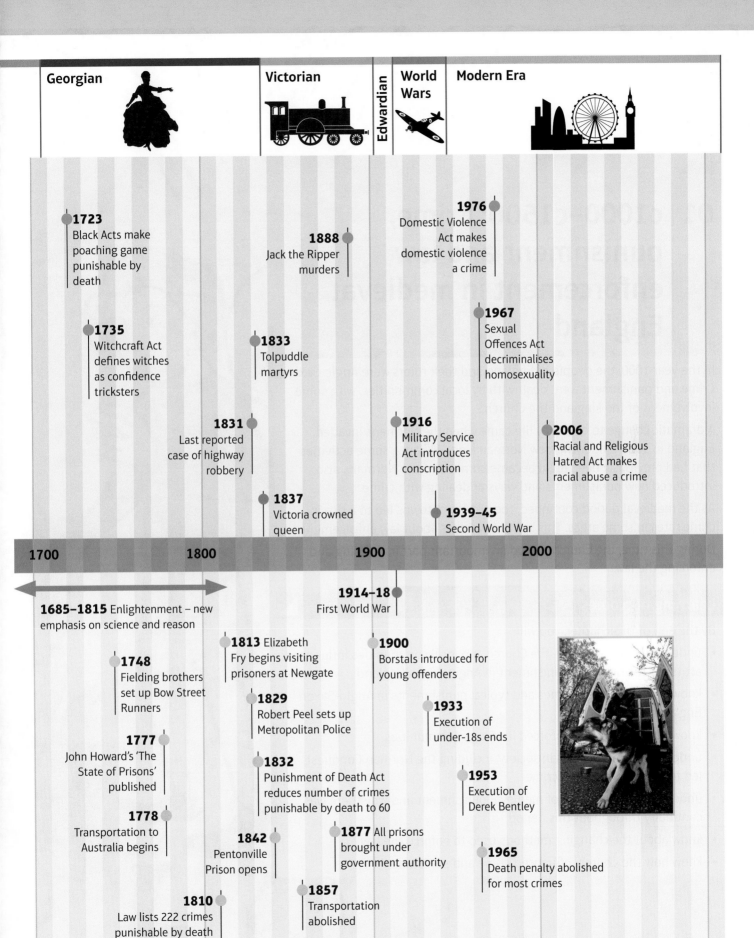

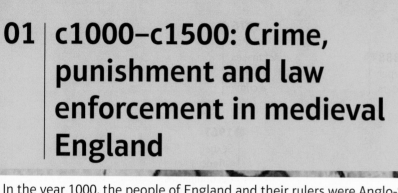

01 | c1000–c1500: Crime, punishment and law enforcement in medieval England

In the year 1000, the people of England and their rulers were Anglo-Saxon. Crime and punishment were dealt with by local communities, with some involvement of the king and the Church.

A dramatic change to everyday life came when the Normans invaded England in 1066. Under the new Norman king, William I, some activities that had previously been legal became crimes and the Normans also introduced new punishments and ways of dealing with crime.

As the medieval period continued, the growth of towns led to a rise in crime rates in some areas. This led to new ideas about law enforcement.

During this time, the Church played an important part in defining and enforcing the law.

Learning outcomes

By the end of this chapter, you will:

- understand how the king, the Church and local communities influenced attitudes to crime and punishment in Anglo-Saxon England
- know about common crimes and typical punishments in Anglo-Saxon England
- know how the law was enforced in village communities
- understand how changes in society, including the Norman Conquest, led to new definitions of crime
- understand the purpose of medieval punishment and why there was continuity throughout this period
- know about the changing methods used to enforce the law
- know how the Church influenced crime and punishment.

1.1 Crime, punishment and law enforcement in Anglo-Saxon England

Learning outcomes

- Know how the king, the Church, and ideas about family, influenced attitudes to crime and punishment in Anglo-Saxon England.
- Know about common crimes and typical punishments in Anglo-Saxon England.
- Understand how the law was enforced in village communities.

Timeline

Crime and punishment in England c1000–c1500

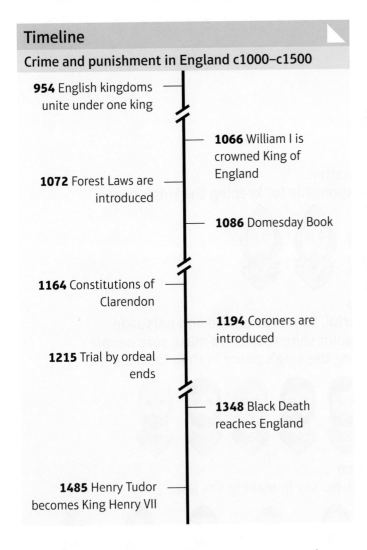

- **954** English kingdoms unite under one king
- **1066** William I is crowned King of England
- **1072** Forest Laws are introduced
- **1086** Domesday Book
- **1164** Constitutions of Clarendon
- **1194** Coroners are introduced
- **1215** Trial by ordeal ends
- **1348** Black Death reaches England
- **1485** Henry Tudor becomes King Henry VII

Figure 1.1 The kingdoms of Britain in c800, before the Norman invasion.

England's population in c1000 was between around 1,700,000 and 2,000,000 and about 90% of people lived in the countryside. The population of Anglo-Saxon England can be broadly broken down into three categories:

- Law makers – the king and nobility decided what the laws were.
- Law influencers – many of the laws and the punishments for breaking them were influenced by the Christian Church.
- Law enforcers – police didn't exist in Anglo-Saxon England. Village communities were expected to enforce the law themselves.

During the Anglo-Saxon period there were three important trends in crime and punishment:

- The power and influence of the king over crime and punishment grew.
- The role of the Christian Church increased.
- The use of punishments, including capital punishment*, increased.

Key terms

Capital punishment*

The death penalty.

King's peace*

Anglo-Saxons believed that it was the king's duty to take care of law and order, so people could go about their everyday lives 'in peace'.

Shire reeve*

An official of the king: his sheriff. Sheriffs managed the king's estates, collected taxes for him and were in charge of local courts.

The role of Anglo-Saxon kings

King Ethelred II ruled England from 978–1016. At the start of his reign, Ethelred had faced conflict in the border areas between England and Scotland, and attacks from Vikings. However, by c1000 Ethelred had more control over the kingdom.

Before Ethelred, communities had made their own laws, so the crime and punishment system was quite basic but increasingly the king made and enforced laws. The king relied on advisers to help him govern the country, but he held overall authority, and it was his duty to keep the king's peace*.

King

Rules the country.

Decides new laws and issues codes of law. Responsible for keeping the king's peace.

Nobles

Given land by the king – wealthy and powerful. Some can advise and persuade the king when making new laws. They can appoint shire reeves* to make sure people follow the king's law. Responsible for keeping the king's peace in their local area.

Freemen

Rent or own a small piece of land. No say in making the law.

Serfs

Own no land – work for others for very low pay. No say in making the law.

Figure 1.2 The main groups of Anglo-Saxon society.

Across England, there was a social structure of nobles, freemen and serfs (see Figure 1.2). All three classes had to obey the king's authority. The king ruled in close connection with the noble families. The king gave nobles land in return for their support.

Actions that threatened this social structure were classed as crimes. These could range from a serf starting a fight with a noble, to what many saw as the worst crime of all – treason*. Crimes of this type are known as 'crimes against authority'.

Crime in Anglo-Saxon communities: towns, the Church, villages

The influence of the church (Moral crimes)

The Church was very powerful and played an important role in crime and punishment.

The Church punished those who broke Church laws, and took responsibility for moral crimes*.

Key terms

Treason*
Betraying the king – for example, by helping his enemies, or plotting to kill or replace him.

Moral crimes*
Actions that didn't physically harm anyone, or their property, but didn't match up to society's views on decent behaviour: for example, having sex outside marriage.

Abbeys*
Communities of monks or nuns.

Crimes against the person*
Crimes, like assault or murder, that cause physical harm to another person.

Crimes against property*
Crimes, like theft, robbery and arson, that involve taking or damaging something that belongs to another person.

Collective responsibility*
In a village community, if somebody broke the law it was up to everyone in the village to take action.

Reeve*
A local official, appointed from the community.

How was crime controlled in Anglo-Saxon communities?

The Church

The Church influenced many aspects of life in the Anglo-Saxon period, including crime and punishment.

The Church punished those who broke Church laws, and took responsibility for moral crimes.

Settlements often grew up around abbeys*.

These communities attracted people to work, which in turn led to more crime.

Towns

As towns such as London and York grew bigger and more important, crime became more of a problem. This was because:

- There were plenty of opportunities to commit crimes against the person* and crimes against property*
- Criminals knew they were less likely to be recognised than in small villages.

Villages

In small villages, most people knew each other so crime was less of a problem.

- The community was expected to take collective responsibility* for upholding the law
- The reeve* would help to enforce the law.

Source A

Extracts from the *Doom Book*. This was the legal code under King Alfred the Great in c893, which was still in force in c1000.

If any one carry off a nun... without the king's or the bishop's leave, let him pay a hundred and twenty shillings, half to the king, half to the bishop and to the church who owns the nun...

If a man [makes false accusations]... let him [pay compensation or let] his tongue be cut out...

If any one plot against the king's life... let him [pay] with his life and in all that he has; or let him prove himself according to his Lord's wer [monetary value of a man's life].

Anglo-Saxon laws

The Anglo-Saxon kings had codes of law. With each new code, new laws could be introduced, existing laws could be changed, and laws that were being ignored could be changed.

Activities ?

1 Look at Source A. Write down examples of codes used to stop crimes against :

   a the person

   b property

   c authority.

2 What do these laws show about attitudes in society at the time? For example, why were crimes against the Church treated so seriously?

3 Using information from the last three pages, create two lists summarising the influence of kings and the Church on crime and punishment.

Anglo-Saxon kings	Anglo-Saxon Church

Anglo-Saxon law enforcement

The way that crimes were viewed was based on Anglo-Saxon ideas about justice and how society should be organised. Anglo-Saxons believed:

- the role of the local community in policing the behaviour of others was very important
- that God was the final judge of innocence or guilt.

The role of the community in enforcing the law

The Anglo-Saxons believed it was a victim's responsibility to seek justice if a crime was committed and that the whole community should play a part in delivering justice.

By the 10th century, English shires* were divided into smaller areas called hundreds. Each hundred was divided into ten tithings*.

All the men (aged over 12) in a tithing were responsible for the behaviour of all the others. One man from each hundred, and one man from each tithing had to meet regularly with the king's shire reeve. Their role was to prevent crime, particularly cattle theft, in their communities. The community was very important for Anglo-Saxon law enforcement.

Key terms

Shire*

A division of land in Anglo-Saxon England. A shire was made up of a collection of 'hundreds'.

Tithing*

A group of ten families in Anglo-Saxon England. They were given responsibility for enforcing law and order in their community.

The whole community was also responsible for tracking down anyone suspected of crimes. Anyone who witnessed a crime could raise a 'hue and cry' – literally shouting for help. Everyone who heard it was expected to help chase and capture the suspects.

Taking oaths

Anglo-Saxon justice relied heavily on religion to decide if someone was guilty or innocent. Oaths* played an important part in proving a person's innocence. Hearings took place in public and the accused* could swear their innocence under oath.

Usually the accused walked free. In small, tight-knit communities it would be very hard for a criminal to get away with a repeat offence. If someone was a repeat offender, or had been caught 'red-handed'*, then they were not given the option of swearing an oath of innocence.

Key terms

Oath*
A formal declaration of the facts, calling on God to witness that what is said is true.

Accused*
A person or group of people charged with a crime.

Red-handed*
Caught in the act of committing a crime.

Petty theft*
Stealing small, low-value items.

Maiming*
Causing physical harm. A criminal could be punished by having a hand or ear cut off, or their tongue cut out.

Trial by ordeal

When there was not enough evidence to prove that a person was guilty, the accused could be tried by the Church authorities in a 'trial by ordeal'. This was a test to see if the accused was innocent or guilty in the eyes of God.

- For a trial by hot water or hot iron, heat was used to burn one of the accused's hands, which was then bandaged; if the burn healed well, this was seen as a sign that God judged the person to be innocent.

- In a cold water ordeal, the accused was thrown into water with their arms tied; anyone who floated was judged guilty, while anyone who sank was judged innocent and pulled out. This might seem unfair, but to the Church it made sense: an innocent person who sank had been 'accepted' by the water as pure – the guilty had been 'rejected' by it.

Christian thinking also influenced Anglo-Saxon ideas about punishments. For some crimes including petty theft* the Church suggested maiming*. The belief was that, unlike execution, this type of punishment gave the criminal time to seek forgiveness from God.

Source B

A trial by boiling water, from a medieval manuscript dating from around 1350.

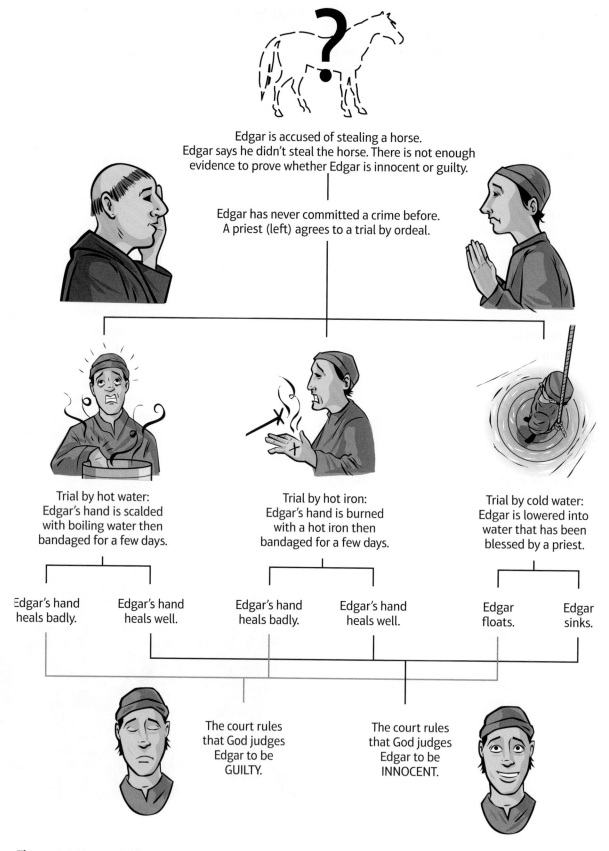

Figure 1.3 How a trial by ordeal worked.

Anglo-Saxon punishments

Murder was sometimes punished by fines paid to the victim's family. The fine was called the wergild – which literally translates as 'man price'. These replaced blood feuds*, in which members of the victim's family sought revenge.

Wergild* was paid directly to a victim's family. A person's class and social status affected how much their life was worth.

Rank	Wergild
Prince	1500 shillings
Yeoman farmer	100 shillings
Serf	40 shillings

Capital and corporal punishment

Some crimes received capital* or corporal punishment*. These were a form of retribution*, but were also used as a deterrent*.

Key terms

Blood feud*
A dispute that develops into a long-standing conflict between rival families.

Wergild*
Meaning 'man price' or the value placed upon an individual's life depending on their status.

Capital punishment*
The death penalty.

Corporal punishment*
A range of punishments that caused harm or pain to the body – including being beaten or having body parts removed.

Retribution*
A severe punishment, meant to match the severity of the crime.

Deterrent*
A punishment that is frightening or painful, and designed to put other people off committing the same crime.

Arson*
Deliberately setting fire to something.

Lenient*
In a judgement, to show mercy.

Treason and arson* (which was viewed as very serious as it damaged the land and property of the ruling classes) were punished by execution – usually by hanging.

For lesser crimes, corporal punishments, including mutilation, could be used. Corporal punishment was meant to act as a deterrent and as a more lenient* alternative to the death penalty. When people saw criminals who had lost hands or eyes, it reminded them of what happened when you committed a crime.

Source C

Skeletons found during an archaeological excavation at Walkington Wold in East Yorkshire. Archaeologists discovered 12 skeletons in total, all belonging to adults, and all missing their skulls. The skulls were later found buried nearby. The archaeologists thought that the heads had been on public display. The archaeologists think this was an Anglo-Saxon execution cemetery.

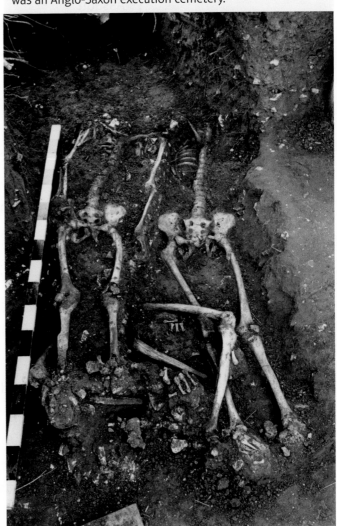

The stocks and the pillory

Some public punishments were painful and humiliating.

- The pillory* locked in the hands and neck (the Anglo-Saxons called the pillory a 'catchneck').
- Stocks* secured the ankles.

Both were placed outdoors, usually at the centre of a town or village, where everyone in the village could see them. People would be left in them, sometimes for several days. Their neighbours might humiliate them by throwing rubbish at them or shouting insults at them.

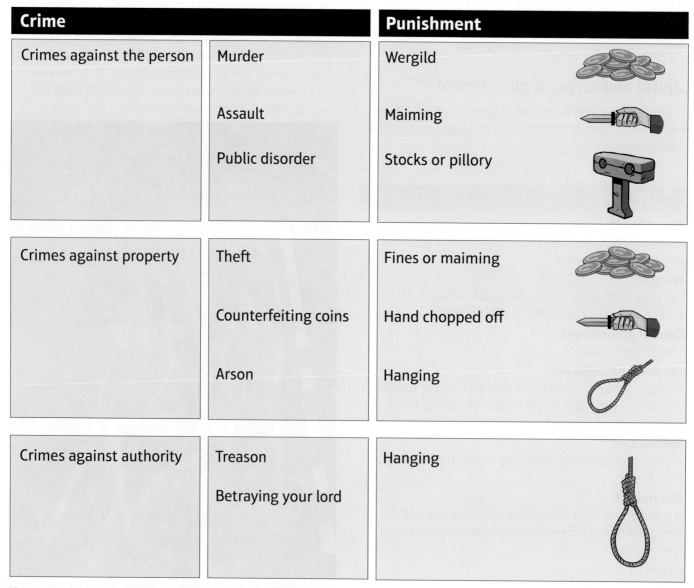

Crime		Punishment	
Crimes against the person	Murder	Wergild	
	Assault	Maiming	
	Public disorder	Stocks or pillory	
Crimes against property	Theft	Fines or maiming	
	Counterfeiting coins	Hand chopped off	
	Arson	Hanging	
Crimes against authority	Treason	Hanging	
	Betraying your lord		

Figure 1.4 A summary of Anglo-Saxon crimes and punishments.

Summary

- Anglo-Saxon kings ruled England. They wrote codes of law and enforced those laws.
- The king was supported by nobles who maintained the crime and punishment system.
- The community was expected to enforce the law.
- Physical punishments and maiming were used as a deterrent.
- The wergild system of fines was introduced as an alternative to blood feuds.
- Some serious crimes were punished by the death penalty.
- The Church was also powerful. It was responsible for trials by ordeal.

Checkpoint

Strengthen

S1 What does 'wergild' mean?

S2 Describe two ways the community took part in enforcing the law.

S3 Give an example of an Anglo-Saxon punishment that would be different for a prince and a serf.

Challenge

C1 Explain what happened in a trial by ordeal.

C2 Choose two punishments from this chapter and explain why they may have deterred people from committing crimes.

1.2 Crime, punishment and law enforcement in Norman England

Learning outcomes

- Understand how the Norman kings increased their authority.
- Know about new laws introduced by the Normans, including the Forest Laws.
- Know about new punishments introduced by the Normans, including the Murdrum fine and trial by combat.

Before the Norman Conquest of 1066, the king, nobles and the Church all had important roles in providing law and order. After 1066, the role of the king became more powerful.

Norman rule in England

William of Normandy (later known as William the Conqueror) conquered England in 1066 after the Battle of Hastings, becoming King William I. Under William I, punishment and law enforcement became more centralised* and fewer decisions were taken by local communities. William's reign also saw more use of harsh punishments, which were meant to help everyone see William as a powerful new king.

Key term

Centralised*

Where power is controlled centrally, e.g. by the king, instead of being shared out.

Source A

An image from the Bayeux Tapestry, showing Norman soldiers setting fire to a Saxon house.

Figure 1.5 The main factors influencing changing definitions of crimes and how these were punished.

The increased powers of Norman kings

Rebellions and the Norman response

Some Anglo-Saxons resisted William I and there were rebellions in York and East Anglia. William's decisions about how to deal with the rebellions show that the role of the king had become increasingly powerful.

He ordered extreme punishments in rebellious areas to show his power. For example, farmlands were destroyed and animals were killed. Some estimates suggest that 100,000 people died of starvation because of the punishments that William ordered.

Source B

An extract from the Historia Ecclesiastica (Church History) by a priest called Orderic Vitalis, written between 1109 and 1141 to record the history of England through that period.

In his anger he commanded that all crops and herds, chattels and food of every kind be brought together and burned to ashes with consuming fire... As a consequence... so terrible a famine fell upon the humble and defenceless people, that more than 100,000 Christian folk of both sexes, young and old alike, perished of hunger.

Activities ?

1 What can you learn from Source B about the punishments William ordered?

2 Describe one way in which William's powers were greater than those of Anglo-Saxon kings in maintaining law and order.

Norman castles

William built castles in every part of the kingdom. Peasant* workers were made to build the castles where their Norman lords lived. From their castles the Normans enforced the Norman law. The castles were designed to keep a careful watch on communities and to look intimidating – reminding everyone the Norman lords were in charge.

Key terms

Peasant*

A poor person living in the countryside, who owns little or no land and works for others.

Feudal system*

A social system created by William I after 1066. With the king at the top, his loyal followers underneath, and the peasants at the bottom, the feudal system helped the king to control England.

Source C

Dover Castle, one of the best-surviving Norman castles.

The feudal system

Norman society was organised around the feudal system* – see Figure 1.6.

King
Owns all the land in the country.
Makes laws. Gives some land to nobles.

Nobles
Given land by the king – wealthy and powerful. Some have castles to help them control their area and enforce the law. In return, nobles supply the king with soldiers and horses for the army. They give some land to knights.

Knights
Live on a smaller area of land. Fight for nobles and the king.

Figure 1.6
The feudal system in Norman England.

Serfs
Own no land – work for nobles or knights for very low pay. No say in making the law.

In the feudal system:

- only the king was free to do as he wanted
- everyone owed money or service to the class above them
- Anglo-Saxon nobles were replaced with Norman nobles by William I
- serfs had to work for their lord
- serfs were not allowed to leave their village – running away was a crime, and punishment for this crime was severe.

Interpretation 1

From *Inside The Medieval Mind*, a documentary presented by Professor Robert Bartlett in 2015.

Inequality and oppression were part of the natural order ordained by God. This was a class system of staggering extremes and every class had an exact price. Just like an animal, a human life could be measured exactly.

Murdrum – a new law

The Normans used the law to control the Anglo-Saxon population. If a Norman was murdered by an Anglo-Saxon, and the murderer was not captured and executed, there was a special penalty known as the murdrum fine. This was a large sum of money paid by the hundred* where the body was found.

Although this was a new law, the murdrum fine was very similar to:

- the Anglo-Saxon system of shared responsibility for the behaviour of everyone in a tithing (see page 14)
- the Anglo-Saxon idea of making a financial payment in compensation for loss of life.

Activities ?

1 Write a paragraph explaining how the murdrum fine was used. Use Interpretation 1 and Source D.

2 Make a list of the similarities and differences between the murdrum fine and wergild.

3 Now compare your list with a partner's. What did you agree on? What different points has your partner made?

Key term

Hundred*

English shires were divided into smaller areas called hundreds.

Source D

The murdrum law, passed by William I in 1070.

[If a Norman is killed] his murderer's lord shall capture the slayer within 5 days if he can; but if not, he shall start to pay me forty-six marks of silver... But when they are exhausted, the whole hundred in which the slaying occurred shall pay in common what remains.

William I's Forest Laws

William claimed huge parts of the English countryside as 'royal forests', which he would use for hunting. After a visit to Hampshire, William took control of what he called the New Forest. Almost 40 villages were thrown out of the forest in order to clear the new 'royal playground' for hunting.

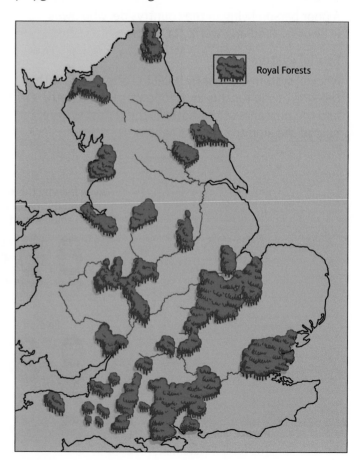

Figure 1.7 Norman forests in England, c1200.

Source E

An illustration of a medieval hunting scene.

The Forest Laws led to great changes in the lives of many in England.

Before the Forest Laws	After the Forest Laws
Some of these areas of England had been common land, meaning peasants had the right to: <ul><li>graze animals</li><li>take firewood</li><li>catch animals such as rabbits.</li></ul>	Many areas of common land were now 'Forest', meaning they were the king's private hunting grounds. <ul><li>It became illegal to hunt without a hunting license. This became a crime known as poaching*.</li><li>Peasants could no longer collect firewood or carry hunting weapons into the forest.</li></ul>

Ordinary people saw the Forest Laws as unjust and unfair. They did not mind if people broke the laws. The Forest Laws created what are known as 'social crimes' – crimes that are technically illegal, but which are widely broken as many people think they are unfair.

The king hired men to work as foresters to enforce the Forest Laws, and to catch poachers and anyone else who did not have permission to go into the forest. Anyone who was caught faced punishments, from hanging to corporal punishments such as blinding. The punishments were intended to deter* others from poaching.

Key terms

Poaching*

Illegal hunting on land that belongs to someone else.

Deter*

To use fear to discourage people from doing something - such as fear of punishment.

Source F

From the chronicles of Abbot Adam of Eynsham, written in the early 13th century.

The worst abuse in the kingdom of England was the tyranny of the foresters... For them violence took the place of law, extortion was praiseworthy, justice was an abomination and innocence a crime...

Activities ?

1 Choose two words or phrases from Source F that describe the behaviour of foresters, and explain what they mean.

2 Why were the Forest Laws unpopular with peasants? Give one reason.

Outlaws and the forest

- Any man, aged 14 or over, who ran away from a trial or a punishment was called an outlaw.
- Women who ran away were said to be 'waived'.
- Outlaws and waived women were not protected by the law – anyone who hurt or killed them, would face no punishment.
- Many outlaws hid in forests.

Myth	Truth?
• Legends of Robin Hood started appearing in the late 14th century.	• In the 14th century, the Folville gang had 50 outlaws.
• Robin and his 'merry men' robbed from the rich and gave to the poor.	• Over 20 years the gang carried out serious crimes against rich and poor.
• They challenged unjust Norman laws.	• It was led by Eustace Folville, whose father was a lord of the manor and probably used his influence to protect the gang.

Source G

Woodcut of Robin Hood from the 16th century.

Exam-style question, Section B

Explain why the Normans made changes to crimes and punishments after the Norman Conquest.

You may use the following in your answer:

- the Forest Laws
- the murdrum fine.

You **must** also use information of your own. **12 marks**

Exam tip

This question asks you to explain **why** the Normans made changes to crimes and punishments. Instead of just describing changes, explain what had caused them – for example, the rebellions the Normans faced after their invasion.

Punishments and law enforcement in Norman England

Continuity and change in Norman punishments

The Norman system of punishment relied on physical punishments, fines and execution.

Change: The Saxon system of wergild was ended by the Normans, and fines were then paid to the king's officials instead of to victims of crime. This increased the authority of the king in dealing with crime and punishment.

Continuity: The Norman system of law was based on the idea that all people should expect to be safe from crime, under the authority of the king. This idea was called the king's mund. This was very similar to the Anglo-Saxon idea of the 'king's peace'.

There was also an increase in the number of crimes punishable by death or mutilation*. Under the new Forest Laws, poaching was punishable by death. Sometimes, mutilation was used instead of the death penalty. This could include branding* or chopping off a body part.

Key terms

Mutilation*

To seriously hurt someone, for example by cutting off part of their body.

Brand*

To make a mark on a criminal by burning their flesh with a hot iron. The mark or brand permanently marked the person out as a criminal.

Source H

An 11th-century picture of an execution by hanging.

THINKING HISTORICALLY ▷ Cause and consequence

The language of causation

There are many useful words and phrases you can use when writing about cause and consequence. Some of these words and phrases can be used to describe short-term causes. Other words are used to describe long-term causes that develop over a longer period of time.

Look at the table below. The first example has been completed for you.

Word/phrase	Meaning	Timing
'Triggered'	This was the final factor that caused the change.	Short-term; suggests the change happened immediately after.
'Influenced'		
'Developed'		
'led to'		

1   Copy and complete the table above, and fill in the blanks.

2   See if you can complete any of the sentences below, using the above words or phrases.

    a   Rebellions against Norman authority .... the introduction of murdrum fines.

    b   The power of the Church .... religious punishments such as trial by ordeal.

    c   William's invasion of England .... wide-spread change to laws and customs in English society.

3   The phrases below can be used to describe how important causes were. Write them out in a list from most to least important.

necessary	contributed to	added to	marginal	fundamental	influenced	supported	negligible

Minor crimes	Punishment	Purpose	Change from Anglo-Saxon system?
Stealing	Fines payable to the king Stocks or pillory Public beatings or flogging	King's authority reinforced Public humiliation Deterrent	Fines paid to king not victims of crime No change No change
Slander (making false statements about another person in public)	Tongue cut out	Retribution Deterrent	No change
Repeat offences	Beatings Maiming Hanging	Retribution Deterrent	No change
Serious crimes			
Poaching in the king's forests, murder, rebellion	Execution by hanging or beheading	King's authority reinforced Public humiliation Deterrent	Poaching is a new crime Murder and rebellion – no change

Figure 1.8 A summary of Norman crimes and punishments.

Trial by combat

Source I

Trial by combat depicted in a manuscript dating from around 1350.

Under Norman law, trial by ordeal continued. The Normans also introduced a new type of ordeal – trial by combat. This was sometimes used to settle arguments over larger sums of money or land. The two people involved in the argument would fight using swords or sometimes large sticks.

The two combatants fought to the death – or until one of them gave in. Anyone who gave in was later put to death because it was assumed they were guilty.

Norman changes to law enforcement

- The local community still had responsibility for preventing crime and catching suspects under the Normans.
- Just like under the Anglo-Saxons, every male over 12 had to belong to a tithing. If one member of the tithing was accused of a crime, the rest of the group was expected to find that person and take them to the authorities.
- The hue and cry was also still used. If a suspect got away, all villagers had to hunt them down and deliver them to justice.
- As most people lived in small village communities, where everyone knew each other, community-based systems for enforcing the law continued to make sense.

Source J

Extract from the Statute of Westminster, passed in 1284.

Thus a passenger would be apprehended and detained all night, and if a suspected person, delivered to the sheriff, and upon an escape, the party is to be pursued with the hue and cry... Highways through every lordship are to be kept clear, for the space of 200 feet, from hedge to hedge, and no bushes, woods or dykes, in which felons [criminals] could be concealed.

Activity ?

Note down two changes the Normans made to crime and punishment up to 1200. Use Figure 1.8 to help you.

Changes in...	Examples, c1000–c1150	What caused this change?
Definitions of crime	**Poaching** – becomes illegal to hunt in newly created forest areas	**King** – wants exclusive hunting rights
	Leaving home – becomes illegal for a serf to leave his lord's village	**Change in society** – the Norman feudal system means serfs must work for their lord
Punishments	**Murdrum fine** – fines for murdering a Norman are paid by community where body is found	**King** – wants to protect Normans against Saxon population
	Trial by combat – used to settle disputes over land or money	**Change in society** – Norman noble custom introduced to England
Prevention	**Death penalty** – introduced for poaching	**King** – wants exclusive hunting rights
No change	Example, c1000–c1150	What caused this to stay the same?
Prevention	No change – **hue and cry** system for catching criminals continues	**No change in society** – most people still live in close-knit villages

Summary

- Norman rule in England after 1066 had a significant impact on definitions of crime.
- William I's harsh response to Anglo-Saxon rebellion, and the building of numerous castles, helped him extend his authority over his new kingdom.
- The Normans introduced new laws such as the murdrum fine.
- The Forest Laws brought large areas of countryside under the king's direct control and made many activities, including hunting and gathering wood, illegal for ordinary people.
- The Norman system of punishments continued to rely on a combination of physical punishments, fines and execution. Trial by combat was introduced as a new type of trial by ordeal.
- Local responsibility for preventing crime and apprehending suspects, through the hue and cry and the tithing system, continued under the Normans.

Checkpoint

Strengthen

S1 Why did the Normans build castles in England?

S2 Describe a way in which peasants were controlled by their Norman lords.

S3 How did the Forest Laws change life for Anglo-Saxon peasants in forest areas?

Challenge

C1 Name two aspects of law enforcement that did not change from the Anglo-Saxon to the Norman period. Why do you think they stayed the same?

1.3 Crime, punishment and law enforcement in the later Middle Ages

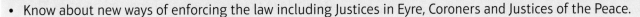
In the later Middle Ages, the government played an increasingly important role in crime and punishment, and the legal system became more centralised.

The impact of Henry II

- Henry II became king in 1154 and introduced some important reforms to crime and punishment.

- In 1166, he reorganised the courts and set up prisons for those who were accused and waiting for trial. These changes were known as the Assize of Clarendon.

- Henry II ordered royal judges, known as Justices in Eyre, to visit each county twice a year to hear the most serious criminal cases. This increased the importance of the king in legal matters, and meant stronger centralised control over the court system.

Change and continuity in crime and law enforcement

In the 13th and 14th centuries, the growth of towns, like London (with a population of 30,000) and York (11,000), meant there were many more opportunities for crime than in small village communities.

- A more centralised approach was needed to control crime – the role of the government increased.

- Rather than local communities, government-appointed officials started to be used.

- Because they were appointed centrally, similar law enforcement methods started to be used in different areas.

- Local officials called 'constables' started to be appointed.

However, for less serious crimes some Anglo-Saxon practices were still used locally.

- Manor courts continued to deal with disputes between the lord and local people.

- Local communities were still expected to help capture offenders. In towns, areas were divided into wards to help with this.

New laws creating new crimes

In the later Middle Ages, parliament* created two new crimes.

- The Statute of Labourers made it a crime to ask for higher wages

- New heresy* laws made disagreeing with the teachings of the Church a crime.

Key terms

Parliament*

In the 13th century this meant a gathering of powerful individuals who met with the king to discuss and introduce new laws.

Heresy*

Actions or statements that were seen as offensive or dangerous by the Church.

The Statute of Labourers

The Black Death hit England in 1348. This disease killed about one third of the population. With far fewer workers available, peasants could demand higher wages for their work. The ruling classes were worried about peasants becoming wealthier and more powerful, and they did not want to pay higher wages, so they used the new Statute of Labourers law to protect their interests.

Source A

Extract from the Cathedral Priory of Rochester chronicle, 1350.

There was such a shortage of servants, craftsmen, and workmen, and of agricultural workers and labourers… [that] churchmen, knights and other worthies have been forced to thresh their corn, plough the land and perform every other unskilled task if they are to make their own bread.

The Statute of Labourers was passed by parliament in 1351. The law introduced a *maximum* wage for workers and made it a crime to ask for more. It also made it illegal to move to a new area to look for better paid work.

The Statute of Labourers is an example of both continuity and change.

Continuity: In the Norman period the ruling class also introduced laws to protect their own interests, for example the Forest Laws.

Change: The Statute of Labourers was passed by parliament, not by the authority of the king alone, as it would have been during the Norman period.

The crime of heresy

In the 13th century and 14th centuries, a small number of people questioned the practices and beliefs of the Christian Church. They wanted the Church to be reformed* and for the Bible to be translated into English so ordinary people could understand it. The clergy* felt threatened by the new ideas, and medieval kings were keen to support the Church against the reformers.

Laws against heresy were introduced in 1382, 1401 and 1414. People who committed heresy were known as heretics. Punishments for heresy were severe, and the 1401 law introduced burning at the stake. This was meant to be a powerful deterrent to others.

The law introduced in 1414 gave Justices of the Peace (see below) powers to arrest suspected heretics. This shows government officials and the Church authorities working together. Justices of the Peace were expected to take suspects to the Church courts for trial. If the Church courts found them guilty, they were taken back to the secular* authorities for punishment to be carried out.

Key terms

Reform*
To change and improve something.

Clergy*
People who work for the Church, including priests.

Secular*
Non-religious.

Activities ?

1   Write one reason why some people began to criticise the Church in the 13th and 14th centuries.

2   Write down reasons why the authorities introduced new laws against heresy.

Maintaining law and order in the later Middle Ages

During the later medieval period, Anglo-Saxon community-based law and order was gradually changed. Two new official roles were introduced – the coroner and the Justice of the Peace. These officials were appointed by the central authority of the king.

Coroners and Justices of the Peace

1194 – Richard I appoints coroners to investigate suspicious deaths.

1195 – Richard I appoints knights as keepers of the 'king's peace' in unruly areas. In 1327 Edward III extended this to all areas.

1361 – They become known as 'Justices of the Peace' (JPs). They meet four times a year to enforce the law. This shows that law and order is becoming increasingly centralised, and how nobles continue to have a big influence on law enforcement.

▶ The development of the roles of coroners and Justices of the Peace

Source B

Extract from a statute passed in 1344. 'Guardians of the Peace' was the original name for Justices of the Peace.

The most substantial persons in the counties shall be appointed Guardian of the peace by commission of the king and whenever need may require... [shall] hear and determine felonies and trespasses [major and minor crimes] against the peace, in the same counties, and inflict reasonable punishment.

Activities ?

1 What can you learn about the authority of Justices of the Peace from Source B?

2 List three ways that the role of government was extended in law enforcement in the later Middle Ages.

Punishment in the later Middle Ages

Punishments in the later Middle Ages continued to be a mixture of fines, corporal punishment and execution.

A terrible new punishment was introduced for the most serious crime of high treason*. A person convicted of high treason would be sentenced to be 'hanged, drawn and quartered'. He would be semi-strangled, then revived, his body cut open, and his intestines pulled out. After death his limbs would be cut off and sent to different areas of the country for display. This was a terrifying deterrent to anyone considering challenging the power of the king.

Key term

High treason*

Plotting to kill or betray the king. This was seen as a crime against God, as well as the king himself, and was the most serious crime against authority.

Continuity and change in punishment from c1000–c1500

	Anglo-Saxon ➜	Norman ➜	Later medieval
Law enforcement	Community responsible for enforcing the law.	Community responsible for enforcing the law. Growing authority of the king and his officials.	Community enforcement continues alongside more centralised systems for enforcing the law.
Punishment	Fines, property confiscated, physical punishment, maiming, and execution by hanging or burning.	Fines, stocks, pillories, physical punishments, maiming. Increase in execution, usually by hanging, for some new crimes.	Fines, stocks, pillories, physical punishments, maiming, and execution, usually by hanging. Hanging, drawing and quartering introduced.

Summary

- Henry II centralised the legal system.
- Towns grew, creating more opportunity for crime and more need to police it effectively.
- The Statute of Labourers shows the determination of the authorities to use new laws to maintain the old order.
- Heresy and treason received harsh new punishments in the form of burning at the stake, and hanging, drawing and quartering – these were designed to deter anyone from challenging the Church or the monarchy.

Checkpoint

Strengthen

S1 What was the Statute of Labourers?

S2 List three ways in which law enforcement became more centralised.

S3 Describe the role of the Justices of the Peace.

S4 What were coroners for?

Challenge

C1 Describe two new punishments introduced during the later Middle Ages, for heresy and high treason.

1.4 Case study: The influence of the Church on crime and punishment

Learning outcomes

- Understand that the Church was influential in all areas of life, including crime and punishment.
- Know about Henry II's efforts to reduce the Church's influence.
- Know how criminals could avoid punishment by claiming 'benefit of clergy' or 'Sanctuary'.

The power of the Church in the Middle Ages

Key term

Convert*

To force someone to change from one religion to another.

The role of the Church

- From c1000–c1500 the Church was extremely powerful.
- It had a lot of influence over change and continuity in crime and punishment.
- Churches and cathedrals were the largest buildings in most villages and towns, reminding people of the Church's importance and God's power on Earth (see Source A).

Source A

At Exeter, this cathedral building replaced the original Norman structure during the 13th century.

What did the Church teach?

- Angels and demons battle for human souls.
- Christian saints were companions who could have a direct impact on people's lives.
- These teachings strongly influenced people.

What power did the Church have?

- It owned one-fifth of the country's wealth.
- It could collect one-tenth of everyone's earnings as a tax.
- It controlled other faiths as well – in the 1290s English Jews were forced to convert* to Christianity or were banished.
- Using trial by ordeal it decided if people accused of crimes were guilty or innocent, and what their punishment should be.

Figure 1.9
The main factors influencing change in crime and punishment during the later Middle Ages.

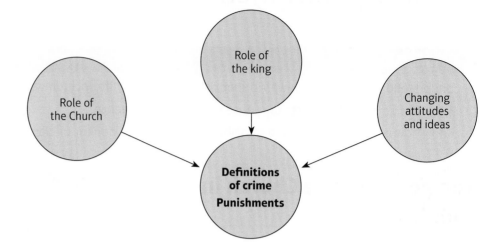

The end of trial by ordeal in the early 13th century

Before the 13th century, the Church judged crimes by using trial by ordeal. However, in 1215, the Pope* ordered priests to stop using trial by ordeal. A new way of deciding if somebody was guilty or innocent had to be found.

In England, the solution was trial by jury. The jury was a group of twelve men who watched the trial and decided whether the accused was guilty or innocent at the end. This system is still used at many trials today. In the late 12th century Henry II had tried to limit the powers of the Church.

KING HENRY II ARGUES
- He should have full power over law and order in his Kingdom.
- Members of the Church are his subjects and should be tried in the same way as everyone else.
- Church courts are unfair and do not punish people harshly enough.
- The Church courts can be abused.

THE CHURCH ARGUES
- The Church is answerable to God and the Pope, rather than the king.
- Members of the Church who commit crimes should be tried in Church courts, known as 'benefit of clergy'.
- Church courts are different as they serve a different purpose – to save souls.

▶ The argument between Henry II and the Church

Church courts and the king

After the end of trial by ordeal in the early 13th century, the Church continued to have an influence on crime and punishment. However, a power struggle began to develop between the Church and kings over who had authority to deal with criminals.

Benefit of clergy

One part of Henry II's argument with the Church was over where members of the clergy accused of a crime should be tried. Should it be in Church courts or in the same courts as everyone else? Churchmen argued they had the right to be tried in Church courts, and this was known as 'benefit of clergy'.

Source B

An illustration from the 14th century, showing a nun and monk in the stocks.

The Church courts only rarely used the death penalty as a sentence, so they were seen as less harsh than the king's courts. Those convicted of crimes would be given religious punishments, such as being told to go on a pilgrimage*, or to confess their sins.

This system could be abused. As the clergy were often more educated, the test to see if they were a member of the clergy was if the accused could read Psalm 51 in the Bible. Many criminals memorised the Psalm.

Reformers believed these practices helped people escape punishment.

Offering sanctuary

Some important churches, such as those on pilgrimage routes, offered sanctuary* to people accused of crimes.

A person who claimed sanctuary could go to one of these churches and ask for the help of the clergy. The clergy did report the crime, but allowed the accused to swear an oath that they would leave the country in 40 days rather than face a trial. Anyone who didn't leave the country in 40 days would be outlawed (see page 24).

Offering sanctuary continued throughout the medieval period and ended in 1536, during the reign of Henry VIII.

Key terms

Pilgrimage*

A journey a person makes to a holy place, often over a very long distance, in order to show their faith.

Sanctuary*

Safe place, hiding place. In the Middle Ages some churches offered people accused of crimes protection from the law.

Exam-style question, Section B

Explain why 'trial by ordeal' was used c1000–c1200.

You may use the following in your answer:

- trial by hot iron
- Church courts.

You **must** also use information of your own. **12 marks**

Exam tip

To answer this question, focus on the reasons why trial by ordeal was used. Try to make a mind-map with two to three reasons, e.g. 'Religious beliefs', and then try to support each reason with some specific details.

Summary

- The Church was an extremely powerful institution and so an important factor influencing approaches to crime and punishment.
- The Church courts provided members of the clergy with alternative trials and punishments.
- Sanctuary and trial by ordeal shows medieval justice often used God as the ultimate judge of guilt or innocence.
- Changes in Church law could sometimes have a direct impact on English law enforcement: for example, the end of trial by ordeal and the introduction of juries.

Checkpoint

Strengthen

S1 Describe how someone could claim sanctuary in a church.

S2 Give two reasons why Church courts could be tricked by criminals.

Challenge

C1 List two ways the Church courts were different from the king's courts. You could focus on the punishments they ordered.

C2 Explain why there was tension between the Church and Henry II over crime and punishment in the 13th century.

How confident are you about your answers to these questions? Reread this section, then try answering them again.

Recall quiz

1   Which three groups (apart from the king) made up the social structure of Anglo-Saxon England?

2   What were the groups of Anglo-Saxon villagers responsible for policing their communities known as?

3   Name two Anglo-Saxon methods for trial by ordeal.

4   What name is given to illegal hunting of wild animals?

5   Name one punishment that could be given for breaking the Forest Laws.

6   Define an 'outlaw'.

7   What law was introduced in 1351, restricting wages for peasant farmers?

8   What crime was punished by being hanged, drawn and quartered?

9   Whose decision brought an end to trial by ordeal in the 13th century?

10 Define 'sanctuary'.

Activity ?

Change over time

Make a large copy of the graph below on A3 paper.

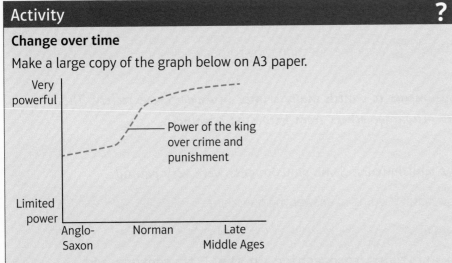

The red-dash line shows the role of the king in crime and punishment.

Add two more lines to show:

• the influence of the Church in crime and punishment

• the role of local communities in law enforcement.

Once you have completed your lines, add notes naming **new laws**, **punishments** and **types of law enforcement** to explain change and continuity on each line of the graph.

WRITING HISTORICALLY

Writing historically: a clear response

Gain more marks and save yourself time by writing clear responses. These activities will help you to do that.

Learning outcomes

By the end of this lesson, you will understand how to:

- use key noun phrases from the question to make sure you give a direct answer
- write short statements to express your ideas and opinions clearly.

Definitions

Noun: a word that names an object, idea, person or place, e.g. 'William', 'king', 'law'.

Noun phrase: a phrase including a noun and any words that modify its meaning, e.g. 'the King of England', 'trial by ordeal'.

Verb: words that describe actions ('William <u>made</u> new laws'), incidents ('the hue and cry <u>was raised</u>') and situations ('William <u>was</u> king for 21 years').

How can I make sure I am answering the question?

Look at this exam-style question in which the key words and phrases are highlighted:

> Explain why Anglo-Saxons used corporal punishments to deal with criminals. **(12 marks)**

Notice the time frame (Anglo-Saxons) and the focus of the question (why corporal punishments were used).

Answer A

> *The authorities used corporal punishments to punish many crimes in Anglo-Saxon society. These painful punishments were used to discourage others from becoming criminals.*

Answer B

> *Anglo-Saxons used many different punishments. Some punishments were very painful.*

1. Which answer signals most clearly that it is going to answer the question?

2. Now look at this exam-style question:

> Explain **one** way in which attitudes to poaching in the 11th century and the 17th century were different. **(4 marks)**

   a. Which are the key nouns, noun phrases and verbs in this question? Note them down then check and compare with a partner.

   b. Now write the first two sentences of your response, trying to use the words and phrases you highlighted.

38

How can I express my ideas more clearly?

One way to introduce your opinions and ideas clearly and briefly is by making short simple statements. Notice how this example answers the question quickly and clearly, while also supplying some relevant details.

> *William built castles at Hastings and Dover. The castles were symbolic of his military strength.*

- The noun tells you who or what is the subject of the sentence.
- The verb tells you what happened.

3. Look again at Answer A's opening sentences:

> *The authorities used corporal punishments to punish many crimes in Anglo-Saxon society. These painful punishments were used to discourage others from becoming criminals.*

    a. What verbs have they used to tell you what happened?

    b. What nouns have they used to tell you what the subjects are?

The writer could have written:

> *Due to the fact that corporal punishments cause pain and harm to the body, they were used by the Anglo-Saxons in many cases.*

or:

> *Many different punishments were used in the Anglo-Saxon period. Different punishments, including corporal punishments, were used depending on the crime.*

Which version do you prefer? Discuss your opinion with a partner. Do you agree?

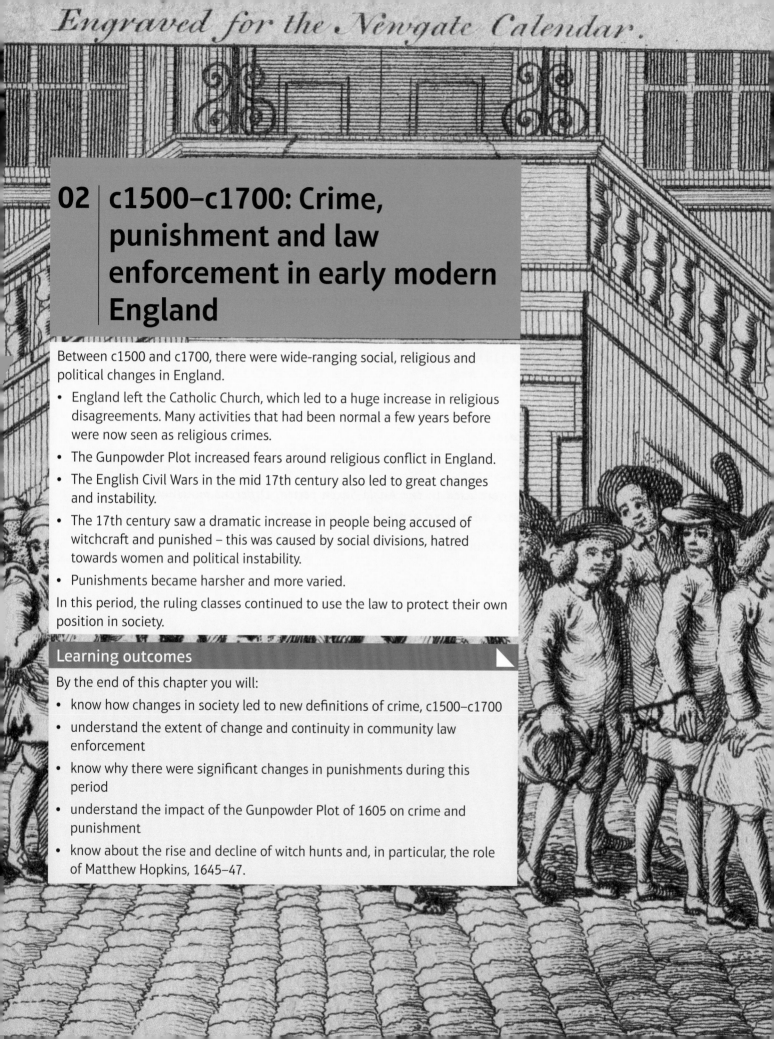

02 | c1500–c1700: Crime, punishment and law enforcement in early modern England

Between c1500 and c1700, there were wide-ranging social, religious and political changes in England.

- England left the Catholic Church, which led to a huge increase in religious disagreements. Many activities that had been normal a few years before were now seen as religious crimes.
- The Gunpowder Plot increased fears around religious conflict in England.
- The English Civil Wars in the mid 17th century also led to great changes and instability.
- The 17th century saw a dramatic increase in people being accused of witchcraft and punished – this was caused by social divisions, hatred towards women and political instability.
- Punishments became harsher and more varied.

In this period, the ruling classes continued to use the law to protect their own position in society.

Learning outcomes

By the end of this chapter you will:

- know how changes in society led to new definitions of crime, c1500–c1700
- understand the extent of change and continuity in community law enforcement
- know why there were significant changes in punishments during this period
- understand the impact of the Gunpowder Plot of 1605 on crime and punishment
- know about the rise and decline of witch hunts and, in particular, the role of Matthew Hopkins, 1645–47.

Learning outcomes

- Understand why the authorities' concerns about heresy and treason increased after c1500.
- Know about new definitions of crime including vagabondage and witchcraft.
- Know about laws introduced in the 1650s banning many traditional entertainments.

Between c1500 and c1700, the changing religious situation in England led to many religious beliefs and activities becoming crimes.

Religious change and changing definitions of crime

Changes affected people in England as different rulers, from Henry VIII to James VI and I, had different religious views.

The different kings and queens passed laws ordering their people to follow the same religious beliefs as them.

This mean that the everyday religious activities of Protestants or Catholics (see the chart below) could change from being legal to illegal depending on who was ruling the country.

Heresy and treason

The two most serious crimes connected with the religious changes were heresy and treason.

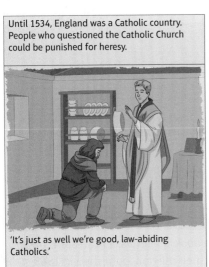

Until 1534, England was a Catholic country. People who questioned the Catholic Church could be punished for heresy.

'It's just as well we're good, law-abiding Catholics.'

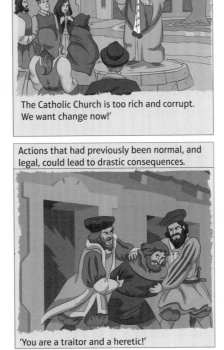

In Europe, growing criticism of the Catholic Church led to a new branch of Christianity – Protestantism.

The Catholic Church is too rich and corrupt. We want change now!'

After the Pope denied Henry VIII's request for a divorce, Henry took England out of the Catholic Church. Henry made himself head of the new Church of England.

'The king is the head of the Church. Those who continue to follow the Pope and the Catholic Church will be punished.'

Suddenly people wanting to follow the old religion could be accused of treason and heresy.

Actions that had previously been normal, and legal, could lead to drastic consequences.

'You are a traitor and a heretic!'

▶ Crime and religion

**Henry VIII
Ruled – 1509–47
Religion – Catholic**

Religious changes

In 1534, following arguments with the Catholic Church about his marriage and divorce, Henry made himself head of the Church of England. Henry remained a Catholic to the end of his life but closed down Catholic monasteries and nunneries and took their wealth and land.

Crimes and religion

Both Protestants and Catholics were punished as criminals during Henry's reign. Protestants were executed for heresy. Catholics were executed for treason because they would not take the Oath of Supremacy*. The Oath required people to accept the monarch (Henry) as the head of the Church of England, or face punishment.

**Edward VI
Ruled – 1547–53
Religion – Protestant**

Religious changes

Edward was brought up as a Protestant. When he became king he introduced a prayer book written in English, allowed priests to marry and made the insides of churches plainer – all these actions are typically Protestant.

Crimes and religion

Some Catholic bishops were imprisoned in the Tower of London. Two people were executed for crimes of heresy.

**Mary I
Ruled – 1553–58
Religion – Catholic**

Religious changes

Like her husband, the Spanish king Philip II, Mary was a strict Catholic. She tried to restore the Catholic Church in England and made the Pope head of the English Church once more.

Crimes and religion

Almost 300 people were executed as heretics for refusing to follow the Catholic faith during Mary's reign. As a result, Protestants called her 'Bloody Mary'.

Figure 2.1a Religious change and changing definitions of crime in England, 1509–1625.

Burning at the stake – the punishment for heresy

Heretics were punished by being 'burned at the stake'. The heretic was tied to a stake (a wooden post) while a fire was lit beneath them. Death was caused by breathing in fumes from the fire, or by the shock to the body caused by the burns.

Key term

Oath of Supremacy*

After 1534, any person taking a position of power was required to declare loyalty to the monarch as the head of the Church of England. The Oath was cancelled by Mary I, but later reinstated by Elizabeth I.

Source A

An illustration from the *Book of Martyrs*, a Protestant book about people killed for their religion, published in 1563. Three women (one of them pregnant) are being burned at the stake.

Elizabeth I
Ruled – 1558–1603
Religion – Protestant

Religious changes

Elizabeth tried to find a 'middle way' in religion. She wanted to create a Protestant Church that was not too challenging to Catholic traditions, so English Catholics would feel comfortable as part of the Church of England, with her as its head.

Crimes and religion

In 1559, Elizabeth passed several new laws about religion:
- **The Act of Uniformity** said everyone had to go to church on Sundays and holy days or pay a fine. Those who refused were called 'recusants'.
- **The Act of Supremacy** reintroduced the Oath of Supremacy. Catholics who refused to swear it were committing a crime.
- Elizabeth got rid of the harsh heresy laws introduced by Mary I. In 1569 there was a Catholic rebellion in the north of England and in 1570 the Pope excommunicated* Elizabeth. After this, many more Catholics were prosecuted for being recusants and hundreds of rebels were executed.

James VI and I
Ruled (Scotland from 1567) Scotland and England 1603–25
Religion – Protestant

Religious changes

James was Protestant but, at first, was tolerant towards Catholics. However, the Gunpowder Plot in 1605 changed his mind.

Crimes and religion

James introduced strict anti-Catholic laws. The 1605 **Popish Recusants Act** forced Catholics to swear loyalty to the king and pay heavy fines for not attending church.

Figure 2.1b Religious change and changing definitions of crime in England, 1509–1625.

Executions for heresy during the Tudor period

Monarch	Reign	Executions for heresy
Henry VIII	1509–47	81
Edward VI	1547–53	2
Mary I	1553–58	283
Elizabeth I	1558–1603	5

Not everybody accused of heresy was burned at the stake. Many people agreed to recant*. They took part in a public display that involved carrying wooden sticks to the place where their burning would have taken place. The sticks were then burnt instead as a symbol of their change in beliefs.

Key terms

Excommunicate*

Eject from the Catholic Church. By excommunicating Elizabeth I, the Pope was saying she was no longer a member of the Church.

Recant*

Make a public statement that you have changed your religious beliefs.

Activities ❓

1 Explain why having different religious beliefs to the monarch was seen as such a serious crime.

2 Describe one punishment for heresy during this time period.

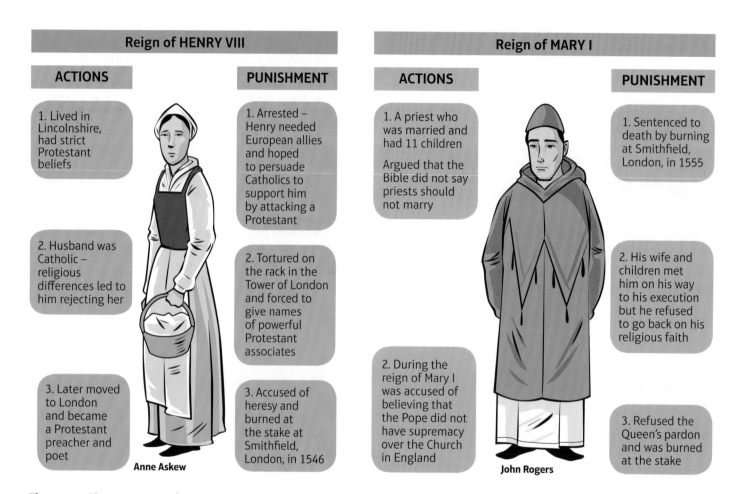

Reign of HENRY VIII

ACTIONS

1. Lived in Lincolnshire, had strict Protestant beliefs

2. Husband was Catholic – religious differences led to him rejecting her

3. Later moved to London and became a Protestant preacher and poet

Anne Askew

PUNISHMENT

1. Arrested – Henry needed European allies and hoped to persuade Catholics to support him by attacking a Protestant

2. Tortured on the rack in the Tower of London and forced to give names of powerful Protestant associates

3. Accused of heresy and burned at the stake at Smithfield, London, in 1546

Reign of MARY I

ACTIONS

1. A priest who was married and had 11 children

Argued that the Bible did not say priests should not marry

2. During the reign of Mary I was accused of believing that the Pope did not have supremacy over the Church in England

John Rogers

PUNISHMENT

1. Sentenced to death by burning at Smithfield, London, in 1555

2. His wife and children met him on his way to his execution but he refused to go back on his religious faith

3. Refused the Queen's pardon and was burned at the stake

Figure 2.2 The treatment of two people accused of heresy in the reigns of Henry VIII and Mary I.

Changes in society and changing definitions of crime

A common view was that vagabonds* were lazy, or had brought their troubles upon themselves.

A 16th-century pamphlet about the dangers of beggars listed many different types of beggar and assumed that none was in genuine need. Categories included:

- dummerers – those pretending to be deaf and mute
- drunken tinkers – thieves using trade as a cover story.

Key term

Vagabonds/vagrants*

A person without a job who moved from place to place.

Timeline

New definitions of crime c1500–c1700

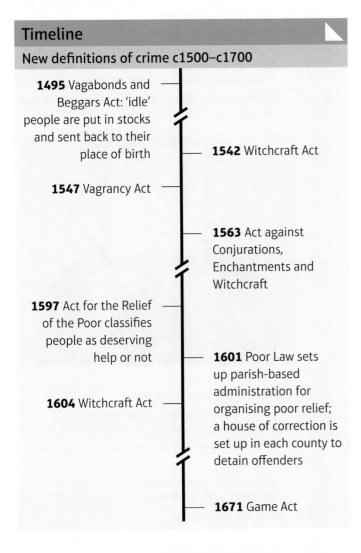

1495 Vagabonds and Beggars Act: 'idle' people are put in stocks and sent back to their place of birth

1542 Witchcraft Act

1547 Vagrancy Act

1563 Act against Conjurations, Enchantments and Witchcraft

1597 Act for the Relief of the Poor classifies people as deserving help or not

1601 Poor Law sets up parish-based administration for organising poor relief; a house of correction is set up in each county to detain offenders

1604 Witchcraft Act

1671 Game Act

Vagabondage

Where did it come from?

- After 1500, people began to move around the country more to look for jobs, due to the increased population, falling wages and rising food prices.
- People who moved to new areas and were unemployed or homeless were called **vagabonds** or **vagrants**.

How did communities react?

It was not always easy for vagabonds to find jobs, some became criminals.

- This made many people see all vagabonds as possible criminals.
- Many people thought vagabonds were lazy or were fooling people to steal their money.

What did the law do?

- New laws were passed to deal with the threat from vagabonds.
- **Vagancy Act 1547**: Able-bodied vagabonds who had not worked for three days were to be branded with the letter V and sold as slaves for two years. This law was so severe it was withdrawn after two years.
- **Act for the Relief of the Poor 1597**: This included harsh punishments to discourage vagrants, including whipping and burning the ear with a hot iron.

▶ Vagabondage becomes a crime

Source B

A 1536 woodcut showing a beggar being punished by public whipping.

The Poor Laws

The 1601 Poor Laws aimed to make the system for dealing with vagrants the same all across the country. All local parishes* now had to provide poor relief* to anybody not physically fit to work. This group was known as the 'deserving poor' and included the elderly and disabled. The 'undeserving poor', who were fit to work, were still punished severely.

This difference between 'deserving' and 'undeserving poor' lasted a very long time.

Key terms

Parish*

A small administrative area, normally connected to a local church.

Poor relief*

Financial assistance for the poorest members of society.

Enclosed*

Fenced off for the exclusive use of the landowner.

Source C

An extract from the Game Act, passed in 1671.

Every person... not having Lands and Tenements or some other estate [is] not allowed to have or keepe... guns, bowes, grey hounds, setting dogs, ferrets... snares or other engines aforementioned.

Controlling the land – rural crimes

Changing times

- In the 17th century, life became more difficult for many of the rural poor.
- Areas of common land that the poor had been able to use for gathering wild food and firewood were enclosed* by powerful landlords, who could make huge profits from grazing sheep.
- Landlords also fenced off large parklands for their private use.

How did this impact the poor?

- Enclosure made it hard for village people to survive. Many left and became vagabonds.
- Some people pulled down the new fences and hedges.
- Many people continued to hunt and fish on enclosed land. This was known as poaching.

What did the law do?

- The 1671 Game Act made hunting and fishing on enclosed land illegal.

How did people react?

- Upper classes and landlords thought poachers were thieves and trespassers.
- Poorer people felt sympathy for poachers.
- Poaching became a 'social crime' – this means many people thought the law against it was unfair and didn't care if it was broken.
- Many people didn't report poachers, making it hard for the law to stop it.
- Many poachers worked in gangs, as this made it harder for authorities to catch them.

▶ Crime and the rural poor

Interpretation 1

From a description of enclosure in *The English Revolution*, by the civil war historian, Christopher Hill (1940).

Some of these poor tenants became vagabonds wandering the roads for bread, so laws were passed ordering vagrants to be branded or to be "whipped until his or her shoulders be bloody"… Legislation treated them as 'voluntary' criminals. Others became agricultural labourers working on the large estates. Others again provided a useful supply of cheap labour for expanding industries. Both these groups were without land to support them in independence in a bad year or when their employers went bankrupt.

Witchcraft

Most people in England at this time believed that witchcraft existed, and that witches could do harm to others, and should be stopped and punished. Punishments became harsher during this period, as new laws were passed that meant those accused of witchcraft were tried in ordinary courts, instead of the more lenient Church courts. For more on witchcraft in this period see Section 2.4.

The rise of smuggling

- In the 17th century, the government introduced taxes on a range of imported goods, including alcohol and tea (a new luxury product at this time).

- This meant a profit could be made by people smuggling goods into the country to avoid these taxes.

- There were plenty of people willing to buy smuggled goods at a lower price.

- Smuggling is another example of an illegal activity that was difficult to prevent, as many people made money from it and did not think it was serious.

Extend your knowledge

The end of the monasteries

In the early 1500s, the main sources of help for the poor (and sick) were the monasteries that were found all over England. After Henry VIII closed the monasteries in the 1530s, there was nowhere for poor travellers to turn.

Puritan rule – new 'moral' laws in the 1650s

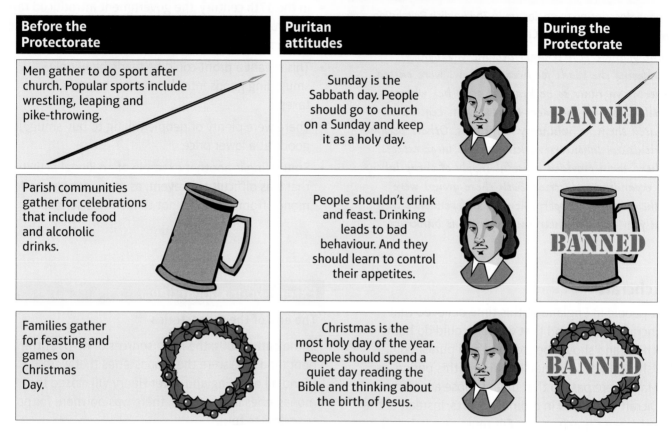

Figure 2.3 Activities made illegal during the Protectorate.

After parliament's victory in the **English Civil War** and Charles I's execution, the leader of the parliamentary forces, **Oliver Cromwell**, became Lord Protector (king in all but name). He governed England from 1653 until his death in 1658. This period is known as the 'Protectorate'*.

Cromwell was a radical Protestant – or **Puritan**. Puritans had very strict religious views. Cromwell thought people should focus on religion and work to have 'pure souls'. Under Cromwell, parliament passed laws which banned many activities that were previously quite ordinary – these activities now became criminal acts (see Figure 2.3). This is a good example of how governments can have a big role in deciding what is classed as a crime. The banned activities did not become legal again until after the Protectorate was over in 1660.

However, in other ways England became more tolerant. The laws that said everyone must go to church or pay a fine were removed in 1650.

Key term

Protectorate*

The period from 1653-59 when England did not have a monarch but was ruled first by Oliver Cromwell and then Richard Cromwell.

THINKING HISTORICALLY Change and continuity (2b)

Events or historical change?

The language historians use can help to show whether they are talking about change or continuity. For instance, 'more' suggests a change from before.

Study the following events and changes:

Oliver Cromwell became Lord Protector in 1653.	More people were burnt at the stake for heresy.	Vagabonds were punished harshly.	More poor people were forced to find work in new towns, and were treated as vagrants.	Henry VIII closed down the monasteries.
The Game Act of 1671 was introduced.	A number of 'moral crimes' were introduced to control behaviour.	Vagrancy laws were brought in by the government.	Harsher punishments were introduced for poaching.	The Heresy Acts were reintroduced by Mary I.

1   Sort the points above into 'events' and 'changes'.

2   Match each change to an event.

Summary

- Religious changes in the 16th century led to new definitions of criminal activity as each ruler tried to impose their own religious views.
- Economic changes led to a big increase in vagrants in the 16th and 17th centuries, and more fear and suspicion of the unemployed and poor.
- The Game Law of 1671 made it illegal for poor people to hunt. This 'social crime' was not viewed as serious by the public and the new law was hard to enforce.
- Cromwell introduced many moral laws during the 1650s – this shows the role government can play in defining crimes.
- In the 17th century, the government introduced taxes on a range of imported goods. This meant there was a profit to be made for those who wanted to smuggle goods into the country.

Checkpoint

Strengthen

S1 Which new 'moral laws' were introduced by the Puritans?

S2 Draw a timeline to summarise the different vagrancy laws that were introduced in this period.

S3 Give one reason why it was difficult for the authorities to tackle crimes like poaching and smuggling.

Challenge

C1 Why can poaching be viewed as a 'social crime'?

2.2 Law enforcement and punishment, c1500–c1700

Continuity and change in law enforcement, 1000–1700

Law enforcement in England, c1500–c1700, was still very similar to the Middle Ages. Village and town communities were still expected to take a leading role in chasing down suspected criminals. However, the growth of towns meant that communities and the authorities had to find new ways of enforcing laws, as the traditional methods became less effective.

1000–1500	1500–1700	Continuity or change?
Witnesses to crime must step in to stop suspects or, if this isn't possible, report them to the authorities.	Witnesses to crime are still expected to try and stop suspects or report them to the authorities.	Continuity
Locals are expected to join the hue and cry to chase suspected criminals down and bring them to justice.	Locals are still expected to join the hue and cry.	Continuity
Town constables introduced.	Role of town constables expanded.	Change
Night watch introduced.	Role of night watch expanded.	Change
No thief takers.	Emergence of thief takers.	Change

Law enforcement: towns

Population change

- Between 1500–1700, the population increased massively from 2.5 million to 5–6 million.

- Many more people lived in towns, which had become much bigger, such as London, Bristol and Liverpool.

- This gave many new opportunites for criminals and it became harder to prevent crime and catch criminals.

Impact on crime

- In rich towns, theft became more common as there were more valuable goods to take.

- Fraud became more common as people living in towns did not know everyone else living there.

- As more people moved to towns, they had less reliable ways to support themselves. Some became criminals.

▶ Why law enforcement became more of an issue in towns

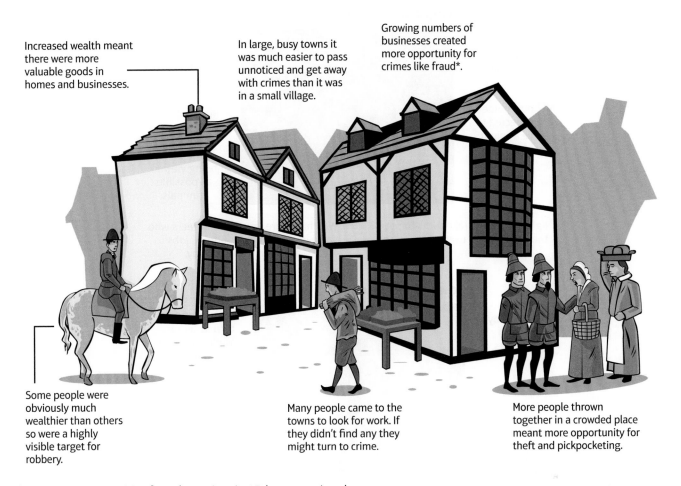

Increased wealth meant there were more valuable goods in homes and businesses.

In large, busy towns it was much easier to pass unnoticed and get away with crimes than it was in a small village.

Growing numbers of businesses created more opportunity for crimes like fraud*.

Some people were obviously much wealthier than others so were a highly visible target for robbery.

Many people came to the towns to look for work. If they didn't find any they might turn to crime.

More people thrown together in a crowded place meant more opportunity for theft and pickpocketing.

Figure 2.4 Opportunities for urban crime in 17th-century London.

Town constables and the night watch

The role of town constables and the night watch grew to cope with increasing crime rates.

Law enforcement at this time was still not nationally organised. This meant good law enforcement depended on where you lived. Householders were expected to serve as constables. Sometimes wealthy householders paid others to do the work for them. In some richer areas, householders joined together to hire armed guards to protect them and their property. These were early steps towards a professional paid police force.

Activity ?

Using Figure 2.4 and the diagram on page 50, make a list of ways in which the growth of towns affected crime rates.

Key term

Fraud*

To deceive someone for personal or financial gain.

Night watchman

Work is overseen by town constable.

All householders are expected to serve as night watchman.

Carries a lamp to help with patrolling when it is dark.

Rings a bell at night to warn people to go home or risk being viewed as possible criminals.

Night watchmen take turns to patrol the local area between 10 p.m. and dawn.

Watchmen are unpaid volunteers who also have to do their normal jobs to earn a living in the day.

Town constable

Employed by the town authorities.

Appointed by local people who are respected in the community, such as merchants.

Expected to turn in serious criminals to the courts.

Expected to stop suspected criminals, break up fights and round up vagrants.

Has some powers to arrest suspects, without the need for a warrant from a Justice of the Peace.

Helps with local administrative issues like collecting payments for road cleaning.

Figure 2.5 The roles of the night watchman and town constable.

Activities ?

1 Write down the main duties of a constable and a night watchman.

2 In pairs, take it in turns to play the part of a constable. Interview each other about your duties.

Professional 'thief takers'

Many constables and watchmen were not very good at hunting down criminals, so some victims of crime used thief takers. The thief taker was paid a reward for catching a criminal and delivering them to the law. However, some criminals also worked as thief takers and turned in rivals to make money.

Extend your knowledge

Jonathan Wild

Londoner Jonathan Wild was a famous thief taker who secretly led a gang of thieves who claimed rewards when they handed in the goods they had stolen. In 1718, he was given the title 'Thief Taker General' and became a well-known figure. His criminal activities were discovered and he was eventually executed in 1725.

Punishment in early modern England

There was a lot of continuity in the approach to punishment from the Middle Ages to the early modern period. The focus was still on deterrence and retribution, just as it had been 700 years earlier (see Chapter 1). In the 16th and late 17th centuries, there were some new punishments (see Figure 2.6).

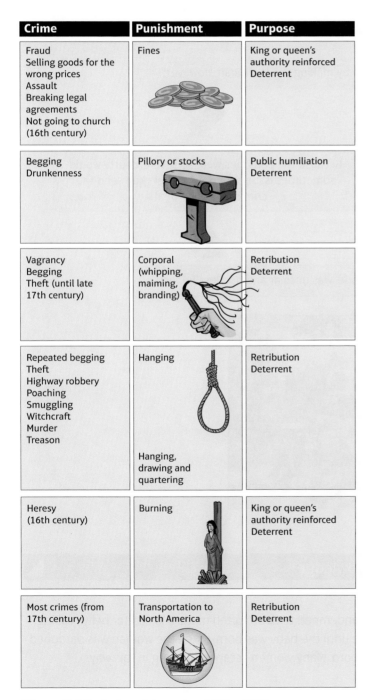

Crime	Punishment	Purpose
Fraud Selling goods for the wrong prices Assault Breaking legal agreements Not going to church (16th century)	Fines	King or queen's authority reinforced Deterrent
Begging Drunkenness	Pillory or stocks	Public humiliation Deterrent
Vagrancy Begging Theft (until late 17th century)	Corporal (whipping, maiming, branding)	Retribution Deterrent
Repeated begging Theft Highway robbery Poaching Smuggling Witchcraft Murder Treason	Hanging Hanging, drawing and quartering	Retribution Deterrent
Heresy (16th century)	Burning	King or queen's authority reinforced Deterrent
Most crimes (from 17th century)	Transportation to North America	Retribution Deterrent

Figure 2.6 Typical punishments, c1500–c1700.

Early prisons

In the early 16th century, prisons often held petty criminals, vagrants and drunk and disorderly offenders.

Prisons were a place where people waited for trial or punishment. They were often a secure room in a local castle or gatehouse*. Conditions were very poor.

- Inmates had to pay wardens for food and other basics like bedding. If they didn't pay, they went without.
- Women, men and children were housed together, and petty criminals and more violent offenders were kept in the same place.
- Younger prisoners were often bullied and abused, or learned how to become more serious criminals.
- Prisons were dirty and unhealthy, with no proper sanitation*; many prisoners died of diseases like typhus.

In 1556, a new type of prison, or house of correction, was opened called Bridewell prison. It was used to punish poor people who had broken the law (for example, vagabonds)

All inmates were made to do 'hard labour' (like breaking up rocks) to pay the cost of keeping them there, and to encourage hard work. During the 17th century, similar prisons were opened in London and around the country.

Key terms

Gatehouse*
Building forming a gateway at the entrance to a town or important house, with a room or rooms above.

Sanitation*
Clean surroundings, clean water and toilet facilities.

Source A

From *Essays and Characters of a Prison and Prisoners* by Geffray Mynshull, published in 1618.

A Prison is a grave to bury men alive... a little world of woe, it is a map of misery... It is a place that hath more diseases predominant in it than the Pest-house in the Plague time, and it stinks more than the Lord Mayers dogge-house...

Capital punishment and the Bloody Code

In the 17th century the number of capital crimes* increased. There were 50 by 1688. Historians call this harsh system the 'Bloody Code'.

Today some of these crimes seem very minor, such as poaching rabbits and fish to eat.

The idea was to have a strong deterrent by making the law harsh. However:

Many people still committed crimes because they were desperate, e.g. their children were starving.

Because the penalties were so severe, courts would sometimes issue a pardon* rather than send the criminal to their death.

This meant the message of the 'Bloody Code' was unclear and had less impact.

▶ Harsh punishments and the Bloody Code

Key terms

Capital crime*
A crime that is punished with the death penalty.

Pardon*
When a person is let off punishment for a crime of which they have been convicted.

Extend your knowledge

Plead for belly

Pregnant women condemned to death often made a 'plead for belly', asking to be allowed to live until the baby was born. Often the woman was pardoned after the child was born. Many women escaped hanging in this way.

Transportation to North America

During the reign of James I (1603–25), transportation*, to the new English colonies* in North America, became a new form of punishment. Transportation was not as harsh as execution, but was still a severe punishment.

Transported prisoners were taken in chains to the east coast of North America, where they would have to work for a fixed period doing tough manual labour – usually clearing trees or doing farm work. After the sentence was finished they were free – but most had no money to pay for a return journey so would spend the rest of their lives far from home.

Key terms

Transportation*
Being sent away from England to serve a period of punishment in a colony abroad.

Colonies*
New settlements in foreign lands – often taken by force from the original inhabitants.

It was seen as an effective deterrent.

England did not have an effective prison system so prison was not always an option.

Authorities liked transportation because:

Criminals were taken far from the people and places that might have made them a criminal in the first place. It was claimed this might help them make a new start.

Convicts could be used to populate and provide workers for England's colonies, helping to make these colonies permanent.

There was the possibility of rehabilitation*. Criminals had the chance to reflect on their crimes and change their way of life.

Historians estimate that from James I's reign to c1770, between 50,000 and 80,000 men, women and children were transported to America.

Key term

Rehabilitate*
Help someone return to normal life and society after they have committed a crime.

Source B

A 17th-century engraving showing people boarding a boat on the River Thames before being transported to North America.

Activities

1 Look at Source B. Choose one of the people in the picture, and write a last letter from them before they were transported. Try to explain their crime, and their fears about transportation

2 Make a mindmap with the heading 'Why was transportation to North America introduced?' Try to include notes under each of the headings below.

- Changing attitudes – new attitudes to rehabilitation.
- Continuity of attitudes – transportation seen as a deterrent.
- Opportunity – new colonies in North America.
- Lack of alternative – England does not have an effective prison system.

Exam-style question, Section B

'In the period 1500–1700, the main aim of changes to punishments was retribution.'

How far do you agree? Explain your answer. You may use the following in your answer:

- the Bloody Code
- transportation to America.

You **must** also use information of your own.

16 marks

Exam tip

This question tests understanding of causation and motivation. You need to focus on reasons **why** changes to punishment were made. To help to plan your answer, make a mindmap with all the different reasons why changes to punishments were made. Start with retribution, but also consider how the need for colonists led to 'transportation'.

Summary

- Between 1500 and 1700, law enforcement was similar to how it had been in the Middle Ages. The community was still expected to take a leading role in stopping and finding suspects.
- Growth of towns and rising crime rates meant new ways of enforcing laws had to be found, and it was increasingly agreed that a more co-ordinated approach was needed.
- The earliest prisons were built in the 16th century and after 1601, more 'houses of correction' were built.
- The usual punishments at this time were fines, corporal punishments and execution.
- During the reign of James I, transportation to America was introduced as an alternative to execution.

Checkpoint

Strengthen

S1 Explain two ways in which the growth of towns led to new opportunities for crime.

S2 List two problems with early prisons.

S3 What was the Bloody Code?

S4 What types of criminals were transported to America?

Challenge

C1 Suggest two reasons why transportation was such a deterrent.

2.3 Case study: The crimes and punishment of the Gunpowder plotters, 1605

Learning outcomes

- Know why the Gunpowder plotters decided to act against the Crown.
- Understand what crimes the plotters were accused of.
- Understand why they were punished so harshly.

Timeline

The Gunpowder Plot

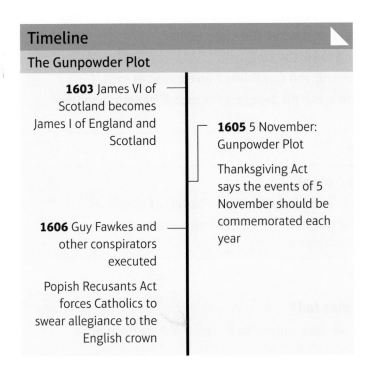

1603 James VI of Scotland becomes James I of England and Scotland

1605 5 November: Gunpowder Plot

Thanksgiving Act says the events of 5 November should be commemorated each year

1606 Guy Fawkes and other conspirators executed

Popish Recusants Act forces Catholics to swear allegiance to the English crown

Key term

Conspirator*

Someone who is involved in a conspiracy – a secret plan to do something illegal.

Source A

An engraving showing the execution of Guy Fawkes and his fellow conspirators, produced in 1606.

Source A shows the gruesome execution of Guy Fawkes – the most famous of the Gunpowder plotters – who was hanged, drawn and quartered in 1606. This type of execution was only used for those found guilty of committing the most serious crime – treason. Guy Fawkes and his fellow conspirators* had plotted to kill the king and so received the most severe punishment possible.

Elizabeth I died in 1603, after reigning over England for 45 years. The new king, James I, was married to a Catholic. Catholics across the country were hopeful that he would allow them more religious freedom. However, James introduced stricter anti-Catholic measures. Many Catholics were disappointed and angry.

As Protestant rulers, both Elizabeth and James were worried about Catholic plots against them.

Activity

Look at Source A and think about what the people who were at the execution could see, hear, smell and feel. Describe the scene.

Why did Catholics want to overthrow the king?

- England had been a Protestant country since 1559.
- In 1570, the Pope excommunicated Elizabeth I and and encouraged Catholics to remove her from power.
- In response, life became worse for Catholics, who were not allowed to practise their faith and were fined if they did not attend Protestant church services.
- By 1605, some were deeply unhappy and began to plot to remove the king.

Who were the Gunpowder Plotters and what did they want?

- A group of Catholics led by Robert Catesby began plotting to kill the king.
- The other plotters included Thomas Percy (a royal bodyguard) and Guy Fawkes, an expolsives expert.
- After the king was killed, the group hoped to replace James with his daughter Princess Elizabeth, who they hoped to control to improve the lives of Catholics.

What was the plan?

- The conspirators rented a celllar under the House of Lords and packed it with 36 barrels of gunpower.
- They planned to blow up the House of Lords on the day of the state opening of Parliament, 5th November 1605, when the king and most of the ruling class would be present.

Why did the plot fail?

- On 20th October 1605, Lord Monteagle received a letter warning him not to attend the state opening of Parliament.
- He passed the letter to Robert Cecil, the king's spymaster, who ordered a search of the Houses of Parliament.
- Guy Fawkes was caught in the cellar along with the gunpowder and was arrested.
- Some historians believe the authorities already knew about the plot and allowed it to proceed so they would have an excuse to persecute Catholics.

Questioning, trial and punishment

- The king ordered Guy Fawkes and his fellow conspirators to be tortured so that they would reveal the names of the other plotters.
- Guy Fawkes was horribly tortured using the rack; a wooden frame that stretched the body until the limbs came apart at the joints.
- After several days of torture, Guy Fawkes confessed and named his co-conspirators.
- The conspirators were put on trial in January 1606 and found guilty of treason. They were sentenced to be hanged, drawn and quartered, a horrible punishment in which the victim was first hanged until they were almost dead. Then, while still alive, the victim would have their insides pulled out until they died in agony. Their head and limbs would then be cut off.
- The horrible deaths of Fawkes and the other conspirators was intended to send out a powerful message about the consequences of treason.

▶ The Gunpowder Plot

Source B

The members of the Gunpowder Plot in a 17th-century engraving.

Source C

An order sent by James I to the Tower of London on 6 November 1605, giving his permission to torture Guy Fawkes in order to extract his confession and persuade him to name his accomplices.

If he will not other wayes confesse, the gentler tortours are to be the first usid unto him... God speed youre goode worke. James.

Activities ?

Make a list of reasons why Catholics wanted to overthrow King James I.

Source D

Extract from Guy Fawkes' confession:

Catesby suggested... making a mine under the upper house of Parliament... because religion had been unjustly suppressed there... twenty barrels of gunpowder were moved to the cellar... It was agreed to seize Lady Elizabeth, the king's eldest daughter... and to proclaim her Queen.

Source E

Documents featuring Guy Fawkes' signatures before and after torture. You can see how weak Guy Fawkes' handwriting was after torture.

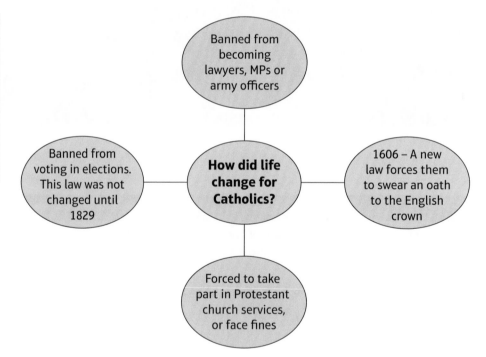

Activities ?

Make a storyboard showing each of the actions of the Gunpowder plotters and what the government did (if anything) in response. What did the government do once the plot had been revealed?

Banned from becoming lawyers, MPs or army officers

Banned from voting in elections. This law was not changed until 1829

How did life change for Catholics?

1606 – A new law forces them to swear an oath to the English crown

Forced to take part in Protestant church services, or face fines

▶ Long-term consequences of the Gunpowder Plot for Catholics

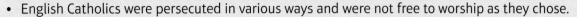

Summary

- English Catholics were persecuted in various ways and were not free to worship as they chose.
- The Gunpowder Plot, led by Robert Catesby, wanted to blow up the king and those close to him at the state opening of parliament in 1605.
- The plot was discovered and the conspirators were found guilty of treason. They were sentenced to death by being hanged, drawn and quartered.
- Following the plot, Catholics experienced more persecution, and were excluded by law from voting and becoming Members of Parliament (MPs) for many years.

Checkpoint

Strengthen

S1 Note down two reasons why Catholics were unhappy in the reigns of Elizabeth I and James I.

S2 Why were Catholics hopeful that James I would introduce greater religious freedoms?

Challenge

C1 Why did it suit the Protestant authorities to uncover such a serious Catholic-led plot?

C2 Why was such a gruesome method of execution used?

2.4 Witchcraft and the law, c1500–c1700

Key term

Pact*

A formal agreement.

Attitudes to witches, c1500–c1700

In the early 16th century, people from all backgrounds believed in witches. Some of the common beliefs included:

- Witches had made a pact* with the devil in return for magical powers, such as the ability to fly.
- Witches were able to destroy crops and to make people and farm animals sick or die.
- Witches had a 'familiar', a demon in the form of an animal like a cat or dog, that helped them to do their evil work.

It wasn't until c1700 that these ideas started to be challenged.

The law on witchcraft

In the Middle Ages, Church courts were used for witchcraft trials and punishments were often not very severe.

However, in the 16th century witchcraft started to be seen as a much more serious crime. Henry VIII and Elizabeth I passed laws that meant people accused of witchcraft could face the death penalty.

Source A

A woodcut showing three witches and their familiars, c1754.

Religion
After Henry VIII became king, witchcraft was treated as treason. Witches were sometimes accused of being secret Catholics too.

The English Civil War
The war, which began in 1642, made people more afraid and this made them more likely to believe in witches.

James I's *Demonologie*
The king was an enthusiastic witch hunter. He published a book called *Demonologie*, which set out his beliefs and included instructions on running witch trials.

Economic problems
In the 17th century there were economic problems such as low wages, unemployment and poor harvests. Witches were sometimes blamed for people's problems.

Vagabonds
The rising fear of vagabonds made people more suspicious of strangers and the poor.

▶ Reasons for the witch craze of the 17th century

Laws against witchcraft

Year	Monarch	Law	Effects
1542	Henry VIII	Witchcraft Act	Witchcraft punished by death.
1563	Elizabeth I	Act against Conjurations, Enchantments and Witchcraft	Witchcraft tried in common court, not Church court – common court penalties more severe. Death penalty when harm caused to another person. Minor witchcraft, using charms and magic, punished by time in the stocks.
1604	James I	Witchcraft and Conjuration Act	Death penalty given to anyone summoning evil spirits.
1735	George II	Witchcraft Act	'Witches' seen as confidence tricksters, and punished with fines and imprisonment.

Case study: Matthew Hopkins – Witchfinder General

In 1645, Matthew Hopkins, a former Essex lawyer, named himself 'Witchfinder General' and decided to hunt down witches in the east of England.

Source B

An illustration from Matthew Hopkins's pamphlet *The discovery of witches*, published in 1647.

In the 17th century, Justices of the Peace (JPs) were tasked with finding witches. Matthew Hopkins was employed by a JP in Essex and East Anglia to discover witchery. There were big rewards, as local magistrates* could pay the equivalent of a month's wages for each accused witch.

The Hopkins witchcraft trials

Hopkins used a number of methods to get confessions. These included restricting the accused's food to a starvation diet of bread and water, and depriving them of sleep.

The accused's body was also searched for physical evidence. Suspected witches were searched for a 'teat' (nipple), which allowed them to suckle the devil's 'familiars' with their blood. A mole, birthmark or any unusual mark, could all be used as evidence of guilt.

Hopkins also demanded that those accused of witchcraft name other witches in their confession. This meant he had a constant supply of suspects to interrogate.

Source C

Extract from the diary of Nehemiah Wallington, describing events in Essex in 1645. Wallington was a strict Puritan who recorded his sins and those of others in extensive notebooks. Here he describes a confession made by Rebecca West.

Shortly after when she was going to bed the Devil appeared unto her again in the shape of a handsome young man, saying that he came to marry her... Asked by the Judge whether she ever had carnal copulation [sex] with the Devil she confessed she had. She was very desirous to confess all she knew, which accordingly she did where upon the rest were apprehended and sent unto the Geole [prison]...

When she looked upon the ground she saw herself encompassed in flames of fire and as soon as she was separated from her mother the tortures and the flames began to cease whereupon she then confessed all she knew... As soon as her confession was fully ended she found her contience [conscience] so satisfied and disburdened of all tortures she thought herself the happiest creature in the world.

Extend your knowledge

Sink or swim

The most infamous method of judging guilt was the 'swimming test' which involved drowning the accused. The guilty would float and the innocent would sink – but, as a result of this method, it was believed that the innocents' souls were saved. However, this method was unofficial and was never used by Hopkins.

Key term

Magistrate*

An official responsible for administering the law in their local area, normally through a court.

Punishments for witchcraft

Historians believe that up to 1,000 people were executed for witchcraft between 1542 and 1736. The most common type of execution for witches was hanging.

The witch hunts of 1645–47 saw the largest numbers of executions for witchcraft in English History. Hopkins' actions made people panic about witches, at a time when they were already living in fear of the Civil Wars.

Women led very restricted lives in the 17th century and were often seen as the property of their father or husband. Women who did not match the expectations of society were seen as suspicious.

Widows, or women who had never married, stood out as being different. They were easy targets for witch hunters.

Many people believed women were more open to temptation by the devil.

As most poor people could not afford to see a doctor, many relied on the work of 'Cunning' or 'Wise women', who were believed to have healing powers. These women were vulnerable to accusations of witchcraft.

▶ Reasons why so many women were accused of witchcraft

A decline in accusations of witchcraft

Some people were never sure about the evidence against witches. They might believe that witches existed but wanted clear evidence of guilt.

John Gaule, an academic, wrote about the lack of evidence at the height of the witch hunts (see Source D).

Why did accusations of witchcraft decline?

By the end of the 17th century, fewer women were accused of witchcraft. There were a number of reasons for this.

- Matthew Hopkins died in 1647, and the hysteria he had helped create began to die down.

- Enlightenment* ideas became more common, and people began to look for rational, scientific explanations for events like crop failure. An important part of this change was the creation of the Royal Society in 1660. The Royal Society gave scientists an opportunity to discuss and share their ideas. Charles II gave the society a Royal Charter in 1662, showing again how the government could help influence people to change their attitudes.

- Gradually, religion and superstition* began to have less influence over crime and punishment. Witchcraft began to be seen as a superstition rather than a crime.

Although public attitudes were slower to change, the last execution for witchcraft in England was in 1716. The witch craze was over.

Key terms

Enlightenment*

Philosophical movement of the 17th and 18th centuries that encouraged people to use reason and ask questions about things they had taken for granted.

Superstition*

Belief based on old ideas about magic rather than reason or science.

Activities ?

1 Read Source D. List two criticisms the author makes of Hopkins's use of evidence.

2 Give two reasons why the number of prosecutions for witchcraft dropped in the 17th century.

Figure 2.7 Estimated numbers of prosecutions for witchcraft, 1500–1700.

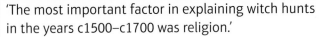 **Change and continuity (3b)**

Significant to whom?

Historians are interested in different aspects of the past and ask different questions. The interest of the historian is a very important factor in their decision about what is significant and what is not.

English historian's focus	Religious historian	International historian	Cultural historian
What led to the rise and decline of the English witch craze 1645–47?	How did religious practice influence ideas about the existence of witches?	Were there similar witch hunts across Europe?	Why were more women than men accused of witchcraft?

Study the following changes and events during the witch craze:

The Royal Society was founded in 1660	Matthew Hopkins operated in Essex and East Anglia	The English Civil War led to greater religious divisions
In 1597, King James I wrote *Demonologie*	The European wars, 1580–1630, saw the peak of witch hunts in France	In 1542, Henry VIII introduced the Witchcraft Act, making witchcraft punishable by death
James VI of Scotland became James I of England and Scotland in 1603	Witches were believed to suckle the devil	Witch trials in Austria led to 139 executions

1   Note down the four different types of historians as headings. Now, under each heading, write which change/event would interest that historian most.

2   Which type of history do you find most interesting, and why? Explain your answer.

Exam-style question, Section B

'The most important factor in explaining witch hunts in the years c1500–c1700 was religion.'

How far do you agree? Explain your answer. You may use the following in your answer:

- *Demonologie*
- the English Civil War.

You **must** also use information of your own.

16 marks

Exam tip

This question tests understanding of key features and causation. Focus on factors that help explain **why** the witch hunts came about and reached a new level of intensity at this time. To help to plan your answer, make a mindmap summarising the main reason why there was such a spike in witch prosecutions during the 17th century.

Summary

- There was a general belief in witchcraft caused by religious fears, James I's interest in witches, attitudes towards women, and the uncertainty created by the civil wars.
- In 1645, Matthew Hopkins, 'Witchfinder General', began hunting down witches in Essex and East Anglia.
- In the later 17th century, there was an increasing demand for a more scientific and objective approach to legal cases and evidence.
- Superstitious attitudes and witchcraft trials became less common over time, but there were still occasional cases of witchcraft accusations and trials after the main witch-hunting craze ended.

Checkpoint

Strengthen

S1 List three types of evidence used to identify witches.

S2 How were witches punished?

S3 Describe one way in which religion played a role in witchcraft accusations.

Challenge

C1 Explain how the following factors can be connected to explain the rise in witchcraft accusations: Matthew Hopkins, the role of the Church, the English Civil War.

How confident do you feel about your answers to these questions? Reread the section, then try answering them again.

Recap: c1500–c1700: Crime, punishment and law enforcement in early modern England

Recall quiz

1 What did the punishment of hanging, drawing and quartering involve?
2 What did the 1601 Poor Law aim to do?
3 What was the role of night watchmen?
4 What was the name of the first house of correction?
5 Name one punishment that was used to humiliate criminals.
6 How many heretics were executed during the reign of Mary I?
7 What was the name of James I's book about witchcraft?
8 Where were convicts sent when transportation was introduced in the 17th century?
9 In what year was the Gunpowder Plot?
10 What title did Matthew Hopkins give himself?

Activities ?

1 Write 10 more quick-fire questions of your own about this chapter.
2 Swap questions with another student and answer them.
3 Correct your partner's answers and discuss any you got wrong.

Activity ?

Make some 'flash cards' for revision. Use different colours to help identify the different factors that influenced crime and punishment in the period c1500–c1700. Use the examples below to help you get started.

INDIVIDUALS	NEW IDEAS	ECONOMICS
James I was fearful of conspiracy. He was highly superstitious and believed in witches. He was affected deeply by the attempt to kill him in the Gunpowder Plot.	The Royal Society was set up to promote new ideas in science and technology. A modern scientific approach demanded a greater reliance on evidence in identifying criminals.	Growth in trade led to more opportunity for robbery.
Matthew Hopkins…	The Reformation…	Enclosure…
Henry VIII…	Puritans…	Developing overseas colonies…

WRITING HISTORICALLY

Writing historically: selecting vocabulary

The best historical writing uses carefully selected vocabulary to express ideas formally, clearly and precisely.

Learning outcomes

By the end of this lesson, you will understand how to:

- use carefully selected vocabulary to add detail to your writing.

Definitions

Noun: a word that names an object, idea, person, place, e.g. 'Mary', 'heresy', 'noose'.

Verb: words that describe actions ('James <u>wrote</u> a book'), incidents ('the plotters <u>were</u> arrested') and situations ('the population <u>was growing</u>').

Modifiers: words that add to the meaning of verbs and nouns, e.g. adverbs, adjectives ('the <u>Bloody</u> Code').

Clause: a group of words or unit of meaning that contains a verb and can form part or all of a sentence, e.g. 'The authorities arrested vagrant children'.

How can I add detail to my writing?

> Explain why vagabonds were treated as criminals in the Tudor period.
>
> (12 marks)

Look at the first sentence of a response to this exam-style question. The key nouns, verbs and modifiers have been highlighted.

> Vagabonds wandered through loads of villages which allowed people to blame beggars for theft that happened.

1. Rewrite the sentence using more precise nouns, verbs and modifiers. You could use the thesaurus extracts below to help you.

wandered through	loads of	allowed	blame	beggars	theft
travelled	a number of	ensured	condemn	vagrants	crime
walked	several	authorised	charge	homeless	loot
explored	plenty of	encouraged	accuse	poor	takings
journeyed	many	permitted	attribute	needy	

2. Now look at the next two sentences from the same response:

> Prices were rising and some people were forced off the land so had no work. People wanted someone to blame for the problems.

   a. Identify the nouns, verbs and modifiers.
   b. For each noun, verb or modifier, note down two or three alternatives.
   c. Rewrite the sentences above, choosing more formal, precise nouns, verbs and modifiers.

How can I make the information in my writing clear and concise?

Compare these two versions of the same sentence from a response to the exam-style question on the previous page:

> Henry ordered that the monasteries should be closed and this caused serious problems for homeless and needy people who could not get any help.

> Henry's closure of the monasteries was a disaster for the homeless and needy.

The second sentence makes the same point, but is much more concise.

3. Look at another sentence from this answer to the exam-style question on the previous page:

> Many of the beggars were accused by the authorities of faking illness or disability and this meant people had another reason to punish them not help them.

> **a.** Rewrite this sentence to make the highlighted text more concise, in the same way as the example does.

> **b.** Compare your rewritten sentences with the original version. Which version do you prefer?

Did you notice?

4. In the examples above, the shorter version has been created by turning a verb into a noun. Copy and complete the table below, turning the verbs into nouns. The first two have been done to help you.

Verbs	Nouns
to build	building
to symbolise	symbolising
to introduce	
to create	
to submit	
to accept	

Improving an answer

5. Now look at the next section of this response:

> Vagabonds were not treated very nicely. They were beaten up in the streets. This freaked out the people who saw these punishments. In the end, people who were caught three times were treated really badly and were hanged as a punishment to put others off committing the same crime.

> Now try different ways of rewriting the sentences to make the nouns, verbs and modifiers more precise. Once you've changed the verbs, see whether you can convert any of them to nouns to make your writing more concise.

03 | c1700–c1900: Crime, punishment and law enforcement in the 18th and 19th centuries

From 1700 to 1900, changes in society began to have an impact on crime and punishment.

- Rapid population growth and urbanisation led to more crime.
- People moving from the countryside to the towns made enforcing the law difficult, as it was harder to keep track of people.
- Poverty in big cities like London, saw the growth of a criminal underclass.

There were also important developments in ideas and attitudes that led to new ways of catching and dealing with criminals. For example, in the 19th century prisons were intended to reform criminals and not just lock them away.

A number of individuals had a significant impact on changes in law enforcement and punishment at this time, including: the prison reformer, John Howard; and the founder of the Metropolitan Police, Robert Peel.

Learning outcomes

By the end of this chapter you will:

- understand how increasing industrialisation and urbanisation in Britain led to changes in the nature of crimes against the person, property and authority
- understand how changing attitudes led to the end of witchcraft prosecutions, transportation, public executions and the Bloody Code
- know about the case of the Tolpuddle martyrs
- be able to explain the thinking behind the 'separate system' introduced at Pentonville Prison in the mid 19th century
- know about prison reform, including the influence of John Howard and Elizabeth Fry
- understand developments in law enforcement, including the work of the Fielding brothers and Robert Peel in the development of police forces and the beginning of the CID.

3.1 Changing definitions of crime, c1700–c1900

Learning outcomes

- Know about the growth in highway robbery, poaching and smuggling during this period.
- Understand why witchcraft stopped being prosecuted as a crime.
- Know about the case of the Tolpuddle martyrs.

Timeline

Changing definitions of crime, c1700–c1900

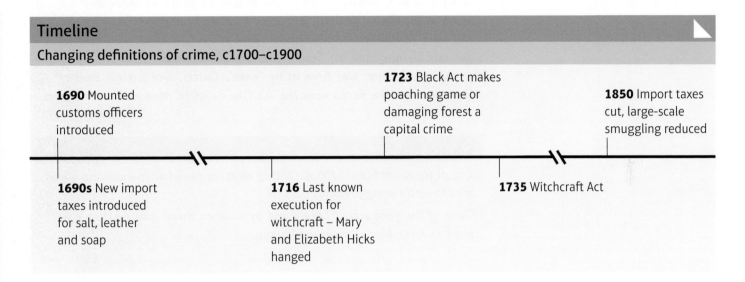

1690 Mounted customs officers introduced

1690s New import taxes introduced for salt, leather and soap

1716 Last known execution for witchcraft – Mary and Elizabeth Hicks hanged

1723 Black Act makes poaching game or damaging forest a capital crime

1735 Witchcraft Act

1850 Import taxes cut, large-scale smuggling reduced

Smuggling: continuity and change

Why did smuggling become more of a problem in the 17th and 18th centuries?

- The government introduced new import duties (taxes) on goods from abroad such as cloth, wines and spirits. This made them more expensive.
- People wanted to avoid paying the taxes, so individuals and gangs looked for ways to avoid customs officers and to smuggle these goods into Britain.

Why was it so hard to stop smuggling?

- Smuggling was a 'social crime', meaning people did not see it as a serious issue.
- Many people, including the upper classes, benefited from the crime, and would not report smugglers.
- Many people actively helped the smugglers, by unloading boats and hiding smuggled goods.
- Smugglers were hard to catch. They often worked at night, and were able to use Britain's thousands of miles of coastline to avoid the authorities.

How did smuggling become less of an issue?

- The introduction of import duties meant that people had an incentive to break the law.
- In the late 18th and 19th centuries, the government cut import duties and smugglers were not able to make so much profit from smuggling.
- As a result, smuggling began to decline.

▶ The rise and fall of smuggling

Activities ?

1 Use Sources A and B and the text on the previous page to explain the methods used by smugglers.

2 Give one reason why smuggling went into decline in the 19th century.

Source A

From a report on smuggling, written in July 1743. The report, which was presented to the Treasury, explains the problems the Commissioners of the Customs faced when trying to stop smugglers.

Henry Dominy Mate of the Sloop [boat] in the Service of the Customs... in Hythe Bay, saw a Cutter [small boat] Commanded by one Jacob Peake, a Notorious Smugler, Close into the Shore at Brockman's Barn, and perceived [saw] a large Quantity of Tea on the Beach, on which he made to the Shore in his Boat and Crew, but were fired at by at least Forty Smuglers, who were Armed with Blunderbusses and other Fire Arms, who Beat off the said Dominy and his Crew - That the Customhouse Sloop coming up to their Assistance, was fired at by Peake's Cutter, and forcibly Beat off - There were on the Beach near the Tea One hundred Men with their Horses.

Source B

A court transcript from c1700, describing what happened when a customs officer tried to stop a smuggler gang.

Three of the gang seized Longly and by violence threw him overboard and tried to spike him... with handspikes.

Highway robbery: continuity and change

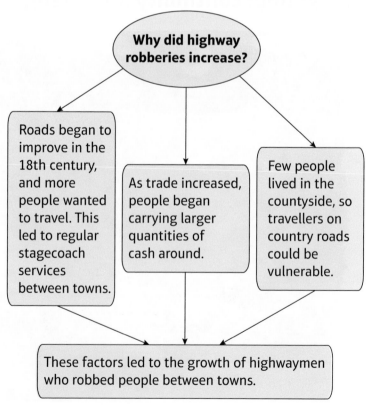

Why did highway robberies increase?

Roads began to improve in the 18th century, and more people wanted to travel. This led to regular stagecoach services between towns.

As trade increased, people began carrying larger quantities of cash around.

Few people lived in the countryside, so travellers on country roads could be vulnerable.

These factors led to the growth of highwaymen who robbed people between towns.

▶ 17th century engraving of James Hind, a highwayman who was executed in 1652.

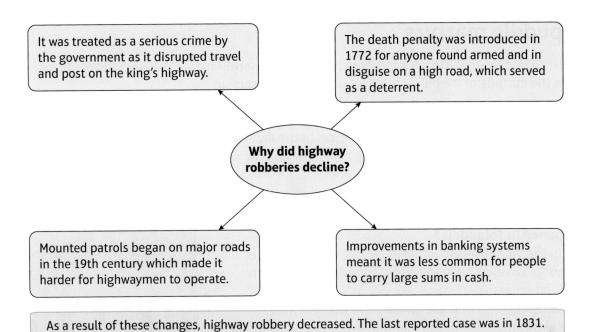

It was treated as a serious crime by the government as it disrupted travel and post on the king's highway.

The death penalty was introduced in 1772 for anyone found armed and in disguise on a high road, which served as a deterrent.

Why did highway robberies decline?

Mounted patrols began on major roads in the 19th century which made it harder for highwaymen to operate.

Improvements in banking systems meant it was less common for people to carry large sums in cash.

As a result of these changes, highway robbery decreased. The last reported case was in 1831.

▶ Reasons for the decrease in highway robberies

Extend your knowledge

Highwaymen – heroes and villains

Highwaymen were hugely popular, despite the fact they committed violent crime. In 1724, thousands of admirers lined the street, from Newgate Prison to the gallows at Tyburn in London, to see the highwayman Jack Shepherd being taken to his execution. The onlookers threw flowers, and public houses gave out free pints of beer. Shepherd had been imprisoned and escaped four times, which led to his fame.

Exam-style question, Section B

Why did the problem of highway robbery increase and decrease in the period 1700–1900?

You may use the following in your answer:

- increased wealth
- the death penalty.

You **must** include information of your own.

12 marks

Exam tip

This question tests understanding of key features and causation. First focus on factors that help explain **why** highway robbery came about, and then on factors that led to its decline. Try to make links between the factors.

Poaching: continuity and change

Poaching continued to be a widespread crime after 1700 and there was a rise in poaching gangs.

- The 1723 Black Act was passed to try to deal with these gangs, by making poaching a capital offence.
- The act also made it illegal to blacken your face (a form of disguise) in a hunting area, and to carry your own snares, or even owning dogs.
- Anti-poaching laws were hated because they were viewed as unfair.

In 1823, the Black Act was ended. Poaching was still illegal but would no longer be punishable by death.

The decriminalisation of witchcraft

In 1736 a new Witchcraft Act was passed which decriminalised witchcraft. People no longer believed in witchcraft and those who claimed to be 'witches' were now seen as confidence tricksters. As a result, punishment for witchcraft became much less severe.

The Tolpuddle martyrs

The case of the Tolpuddle martyrs* is a good example of how the government dealt with threats to authority at this time, and how the attitude of the public could influence the government.

Impact of the French Revolution
- In 1789, the French government was overthrown in the French Revolution, leading to violence and chaos.
- Many people were worried that something similar might happen in Britain.

What happened in Tolpuddle?
- In 1834, in the village of Tolpuddle in Devon, a farm labourer called George Loveless tried to form a 'friendly society' with five other labourers.
- This was an early form of trade union*. The workers were unhappy about their low wages and wanted to put pressure on their employers to pay them more.
- The authorities, alarmed at what they regarded as troublemaking behaviour, ordered the arrests of the men under an old law intended to stop mutinies* in the Navy.

▶ A 19th century illustration of the Tolpuddle Martyrs

What sentence were the men given?
- The men were given the most extreme sentence available to the judge – they were sent (transported) to Australia for seven years.
- This was intended to deter others from trying to form trade unions.

Public reaction
- Newspapers helped to spread the news of the sentencing, creating public outrage.
- In London, 100,000 people gathered to protest about the sentence. A petition with 200,000 names was presented to parliament.

Government reaction
- Initially, the Home Secretary* Lord Melbourne ignored the protests.
- However, four years later the government pardoned the men. When they returned home they received a 'hero's welcome' from the public.

▶ Public pressure and the Tolpuddle martyrs

Source C

This article about the trial of the Tolpuddle martyrs is from the *Caledonian Mercury* newspaper, published 29 March 1834.

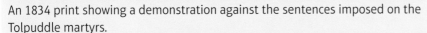

TRADES' UNIONS.—At the Dorchester Assizes on Monday, six labourers, named J. Loveless, J. Loveless, T. Stanfield, J. Stanfield, J. Hammett, and J. Brine, were indicted under the 57th Geo. III. c. 19, sec. 25, for having administered an unlawful oath to John Lock. The prisoners belonged to the "Friendly Society of Agricultural Labourers," which contained provisions among its rules, that if any master attempted to reduce the wages of his workmen, those who were members of the society should quit, and that no member should divulge any of the secrets, or violate the same ; and that if he did, his crime would be communicated to all the lodges in the country, and he would be hunted from the society of the Unionists. Two men, named Lock and Legg, gave evidence that they had joined the Union, and that they were blindfolded in a room at a house in Tolpuddle, and sworn to strike for wages when others did, and to wish that their " souls might be plunged into eternity " if they divulged the secrets of the order. After the ceremony, the handkerchief was removed from their eyes, and they were told to look on the picture of a skeleton, some one exclaiming at the time, " Remember your end." Mr Baron Williams said, that if the Jury were satisfied that the oath was intended as an obligation on the conscience of the person taking it, it came within the meaning of the act, and the prisoners must be found guilty. The Jury returned a verdict of *Guilty*, and all the prisoners were sentenced to be transported for seven years.

Extend your knowledge

A time of change

There were huge changes in working and urban life for many of England's people at the end of the 18th and beginning of the 19th centuries. Many of those working in the new industries lived in poor conditions, had low wages and little legal protection as workers. Some working people started to demand changes to the political system, such as the right to vote and the right to go on strike. Some workers formed trade unions to campaign for greater rights and improved conditions. Those in power were concerned that this could lead to too much power being in the hands of the workers.

Key terms

Martyr*
A person who suffers for their beliefs and, often, is admired for it.

Trade union*
An organisation that represents workers to protect their rights.

Mutiny*
When sailors try to take control of the ship from the captain.

Home Secretary*
The government minister with responsibility for law and order.

Source D

An 1834 print showing a demonstration against the sentences imposed on the Tolpuddle martyrs.

THINKING HISTORICALLY — Change and continuity (3a)

Cause and consequence

Historians need to be able to divide events/factors into causes and consequences. Look at the examples below.

The Tolpuddle martyrs

Early trade unions were set up in the 1830s.	The government was concerned about revolutionary ideas spreading from France to England.	Farm labourers in England were poorly paid.	The Tolpuddle martyrs were transported to Australia.
The government was prepared to use the law to protect the interests of employers.	There were huge protests about the punishment of the Tolpuddle martyrs.	The Tolpuddle martyrs inspired many workers, in the long term, to fight for better workers' rights.	The Tolpuddle martyrs' punishment was repealed and they were pardoned.

1 Decide which of the factors above are causes, and which are consequences.

2 Design a flowchart showing the causes and consequences in rough chronological order.

Summary

- Smuggling increased in the 18th century, while there were good profits to be made – then became less common in the 19th century, as it became less profitable.
- Highway robbery became less common as new mounted patrols clamped down on robbers.
- Increasingly harsh and unpopular laws were passed against poaching. They were repealed in the 1820s.
- The case of the Tolpuddle martyrs shows how what was viewed as criminal activity could change over time.

Checkpoint

Strengthen

S1 What crime was the Black Act meant to tackle?

S2 What crime was committed by the Tolpuddle martyrs?

S3 Why were the Tolpuddle martyrs eventually pardoned?

Challenge

C1 Give two reasons why poaching was treated as such a serious crime.

C2 Why were highwaymen treated as heroes by some people?

How confident do you feel about your answers to these questions? Form a small group and discuss any answers you are not sure about. Look for the answers in this section. Now rewrite your answers as a group.

Learning outcomes

- Understand why there was a decline in the use of the death penalty.
- Know why transportation to Australia was introduced and later ended.
- Know why the use of execution in public was ended.
- Understand changes in the use of prison as a punishment.

Timeline

Punishment c1700–c1900

1713 Stealing more than 40 shillings from a home becomes a capital offence

1723 Black Act makes poaching game or damaging forest a capital crime

1778 Transportation to Australia introduced

1810 222 crimes are capital offences

1814 Last hanging under the Black Act (for cutting down an orchard)

1822 Last hanging for shoplifting

1832 Punishment of Death Act reduces number of capital crimes to 60

1823 Judgement of Death Act gives judges power to reduce death penalty to transportation or imprisonment (except for treason or murder)

1850 National Prison Department takes overall control of prison system

1868 Capital Punishment Amendment Act ends public execution

1902 Holloway Prison for women opens

1902 Executions move from Newgate to Pentonville Prison

Decline of the death penalty

Between 1688 and 1810, the number of crimes punishable by death rose from 50 to 222. However, by the 19th century the Bloody Code (see Chapter 2) was increasingly questioned, and many people believed other punishments should be found.

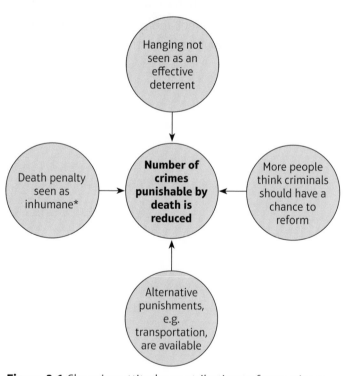

Figure 3.1 Changing attitudes contributing to fewer crimes being punishable by death.

Key term

Inhumane*

Cruel, without compassion.

Transportation to Australia

From the 17th century onwards, the lack of prisons in Britain, combined with the need for labour in Britain's colonies, led to a new form of punishment – transportation. Thousands of people were punished in this way between the 17th and 19th centuries.

For many, transportation meant that they would never see their families or homeland again.

Source A

This cartoon was printed in the humorous magazine, *Punch*, in 1864.

COLONISTS AND CONVICTS.

AUSTRALIAN COLONIST. "NOW, MR. BULL! DON'T SHOOT ANY MORE OF YOUR *RUBBISH* HERE, OR YOU AND I SHALL QUARREL."

The beginning of transportation
- Transportation was first used as a punishment in 1610, when convicts were sent to the new colonies in North America.
- When the colonies were lost after Britain's defeat in the American War of Independence in 1783, prisoners were sent to Australia instead.
- About 160,000 people were transported to Australia. A sixth of them were women.

Why was transportation used as a punishment?
- Transportation was seen as an effective deterrent, and a more humane alternative to the death penalty.
- It also saved Britain the expense and effort of having to send people to prison, and provided a free source of labour for the new colonies.
- Transportation was seen as a good punishment for petty crimes such as theft.

What was transportation like?
- After their trial, prisoners were often held in disused ships known as prison 'hulks'. Conditions were harsh and prisoners were kept in chains.
- On the voyage to Australia, prisoners were kept below deck in cramped conditions. The journey could take three months.
- Once in Australia, settlers were forced to work. They were provided with basic food and housing.
- A prisoner's sentence was supposed to last for seven years, but many could not afford to return home so stayed in Australia.

Why did transportation come to an end?
Transportation officially ended in 1868. This was due to changing attitudes in both Britain and Australia.

In Australia:

- People resented the convicts as they believed they created high levels of crime, drove down wages and took up jobs.

In Britain:

- Some people felt transportation was too hard on prisoners. Other people felt it was too soft on prisoners.
- Many people wanted to move to Australia so being transported there became less of a deterrent.
- More prison places were available at home, reducing the need for transportation.

Exam-style question, Section B

Why was transportation used as a punishment in the period c1600–c1850? You may use the following in your answer:

- American colonies
- convict labourers.

You **must** include information of your own.

12 marks

Exam tip

To answer this question you need to think about the range of different reasons why this punishment was used. Break it down into separate sections, dealing with transportation to America and then to Australia. Explain how different factors connect as you build your argument.

The end of public executions

During the 19th century, calls for public executions to end increased. Some of the reasons given were:

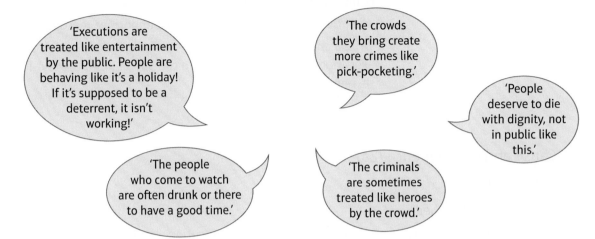

'Executions are treated like entertainment by the public. People are behaving like it's a holiday! If it's supposed to be a deterrent, it isn't working!'

'The crowds they bring create more crimes like pick-pocketing.'

'People deserve to die with dignity, not in public like this.'

'The people who come to watch are often drunk or there to have a good time.'

'The criminals are sometimes treated like heroes by the crowd.'

The last public execution took place in 1868. From then on, executions were carried out in private.

Source B

'The Idle 'Prentice Executed at Tyburn', engraved by the British artist William Hogarth, in 1747. The Tyburn tree is in the distance. While the hanging takes place the crowd are rioting and further crimes are being committed.

Extend your knowledge

The Tyburn tree

The most famous area where public executions took place was at Tyburn (now Marble Arch) in London. The Tyburn tree ultimately developed into a man-made gibbet (scaffold) large enough to hang 24 people at once, on what were known as 'hanging days'. These days attracted crowds of thousands.

Source C

Extract from a letter from the novelist Charles Dickens to the *Daily News*, written in 1846 after he had attended a public hanging.

No sorrow, no salutary terror, no abhorrence, no seriousness; nothing but ribaldry, debauchery, levity, drunkenness, and flaunting vice in fifty other shapes.

Activities	?

1   Make a list summarising the reasons why public executions were banned in the 19th century.

2   What do you think were the two most important reasons?

3   Write a speech from Charles Dickens about his opposition to public executions. Use information from the Sources and the text in this section.

THINKING HISTORICALLY   Cause and Consequence (2a)

The web of multiple causes

Why was public execution abolished?

Study these causes which would help historians to explain why public execution was abolished:

High-profile individuals openly criticised public execution.	The public appeared to watch public executions in a light-hearted way.	The large crowds that gathered at public executions led to more opportunities for crime.
Sometimes the convict was treated as a hero by the crowd.	Policing the crowds was difficult and expensive.	Public executions did not appear to reduce crime.

Work in pairs. Take an A3 sheet of paper. You will need to use all of this.

1   Write two of the causes on the paper, with some space between them.

2   Think of anything that connects the causes. Draw a line between them and describe the connection by writing along the line.

3   Add all the other causes in turn and make as many links as you can with other causes.

4   Now add the outcome to the diagram: 'Public executions were ended'. Think carefully about where to place this and how it should be linked into the diagram of causes.

Answer the following:

5   Can your diagram help you to work out which causes were more important?

6   Write a paragraph explaining why the government ended public executions. Make sure you mention all the causes in the table. Use the links you have identified between the causes to help you.

Prison reform

The changing role of prisons

Before the 18th century, prisons were mostly used to hold people before trial or while they were waiting for punishment. Conditions were very poor (see Chapter 2, page 53).

During the 18th and 19th centuries, imprisonment was used more and more as a punishment. This was due to the decline of the Bloody Code and concerns about transportation. Common views of prison were:

- it was an opportunity to change or help a criminal get back to a more normal life (rehabilitate)
- a prison term should deter others from crime
- prison sentences should involve hard work to pay back society
- prison made society safer by separating criminals from everyone else.

Some people thought prisons should focus on punishment. They felt prisoners should be kept in harsh conditions and do hard labour.

A common hard labour was the treadwheel. Prisoners walked on the wheel for ten minutes, followed by a short five-minute break, for eight hours a day. Prisoners climbed over 2.5km every day. They were kept in separate booths so they couldn't talk to each other. The treadwheel helped generate power, which was sometimes used in the prison.

Prison reformers generally thought that the main purpose of prison should be rehabilitation*. Two of the most influential reformers were John Howard and Elizabeth Fry.

> **Key term**
>
> **Rehabilitation***
>
> Helping people to make changes in their lives, in this case to help them find new skills and jobs to stop them from being criminals.

Source D

A row of treadwheels at Pentonville Prison, photographed in 1895.

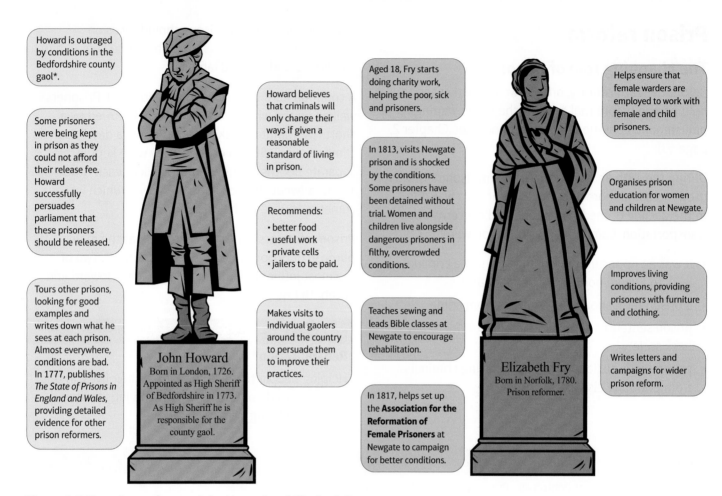

Howard is outraged by conditions in the Bedfordshire county gaol*.

Some prisoners were being kept in prison as they could not afford their release fee. Howard successfully persuades parliament that these prisoners should be released.

Tours other prisons, looking for good examples and writes down what he sees at each prison. Almost everywhere, conditions are bad. In 1777, publishes *The State of Prisons in England and Wales*, providing detailed evidence for other prison reformers.

Howard believes that criminals will only change their ways if given a reasonable standard of living in prison.

Recommends:
• better food
• useful work
• private cells
• jailers to be paid.

Makes visits to individual gaolers around the country to persuade them to improve their practices.

John Howard
Born in London, 1726. Appointed as High Sheriff of Bedfordshire in 1773. As High Sheriff he is responsible for the county gaol.

Aged 18, Fry starts doing charity work, helping the poor, sick and prisoners.

In 1813, visits Newgate prison and is shocked by the conditions. Some prisoners have been detained without trial. Women and children live alongside dangerous prisoners in filthy, overcrowded conditions.

Teaches sewing and leads Bible classes at Newgate to encourage rehabilitation.

In 1817, helps set up the **Association for the Reformation of Female Prisoners** at Newgate to campaign for better conditions.

Helps ensure that female warders are employed to work with female and child prisoners.

Organises prison education for women and children at Newgate.

Improves living conditions, providing prisoners with furniture and clothing.

Writes letters and campaigns for wider prison reform.

Elizabeth Fry
Born in Norfolk, 1780. Prison reformer.

Figure 3.2 The prison reformers John Howard and Elizabeth Fry.

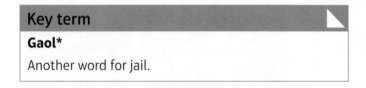

Key term

Gaol*

Another word for jail.

Growing government involvement

During this period, the government became increasingly involved in the organisation and running of the prison system. See Section 3.4, to find out more about how the new rules were applied at Pentonville Prison.

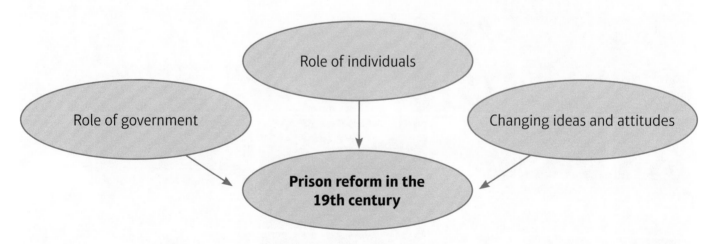

Figure 3.3 Factors influencing prison reform in the 19th century.

Timeline

Reorganising the prison system, 1815–77

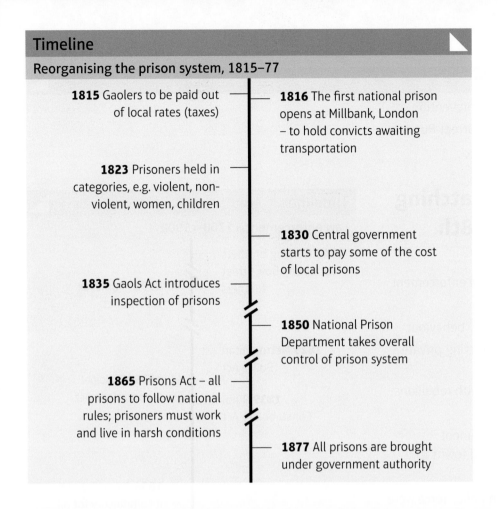

1815 Gaolers to be paid out of local rates (taxes)

1816 The first national prison opens at Millbank, London – to hold convicts awaiting transportation

1823 Prisoners held in categories, e.g. violent, non-violent, women, children

1830 Central government starts to pay some of the cost of local prisons

1835 Gaols Act introduces inspection of prisons

1850 National Prison Department takes overall control of prison system

1865 Prisons Act – all prisons to follow national rules; prisoners must work and live in harsh conditions

1877 All prisons are brought under government authority

Summary

- During the early part of the 19th century, the Bloody Code was questioned by those who believed more effective punishments should be found for less serious crimes.
- Transportation to Australia was a serious punishment and was seen as an effective deterrent.
- Reformers, such as Charles Dickens, questioned whether the public execution of criminals was an effective deterrent and led campaigns to change opinions.
- The growth of the prison system meant an alternative punishment to transportation was available.

Checkpoint

Strengthen

S1 List two criticisms that Elizabeth Fry made of prisons.

S2 Write down three factors that led to the decline of the Bloody Code.

Challenge

C1 Australia and Britain criticised transportation for different reasons. Give one example of a difference.

C2 Explain why either Elizabeth Fry or John Howard was an important figure in the reform of punishments.

How confident do you feel about your answers to these questions? Reread the section, making notes as you go. Now try answering the questions again.

3.3 Law enforcement, c1700–c1900

Crime prevention and catching criminals in the early 18th century

In the early 18th century, methods of law enforcement were similar to previous centuries.

- Parish constables dealt with disorderly behaviour.
- Watchmen were responsible for protecting private property.
- Part-time soldiers were used to deal with rebellions or riots.

However, some towns had paid for permanent constables and watchmen, who patrolled towns to prevent crime and to arrest suspects.

Therefore, some features of a modern police force were already in place.

Timeline
Law enforcement, c1700–c1900

1748 Fielding brothers set up the Bow Street Runners

1792 Middlesex Justices Act

1829 Metropolitan Police Act

1835 Municipal Corporations Act

1839 Rural Constabulary Act

1856 Police Act makes it compulsory for all towns and counties to set up a police force

1869 National Crime Records established

1878 Criminal Investigations Department (CID) set up

1902 First conviction in court using fingerprint evidence

1748–19th century: From the Bow Street Runners to a professional police force

The formation of the Bow Street Runners

- In 1748, Henry Fielding, who was a famous author and magistrate in London, began operating a team of 'thief takers' on Bow Street to enforce the law. The team became known as the Bow Street Runners.
- In 1754, Henry's brother John Fielding took over the Bow Street Runners.
- At first, they funded themselves by charging fees and collecting rewards. However, in 1785 they were funded by the government, and became the first modern detective force.
- The Bow Street Runners' approach paved the way for the future. Their methods deterred crime and also made it easier to catch criminals. They understood the importance of collecting and sharing intelligence to catch criminals.

Steps towards a professional police force

- Inspired by the example of the Fielding brothers, other detective offices were created in Middlesex and Westminster.
- In 1792, the Middlesex Justices Act set up further offices, with six constables given the job of detecting and arresting suspects.
- By the beginning of the 19th century, it became clear the old system of part-time constables and watchmen could not continue.

Source A

A popular print, published in 1806, showing the Bow Street Runners catching criminals.

London's first professional police force

- In 1829, the Home Secretary Robert Peel helped pass the Metropolitan Police Act, which created the world's first professional police force – the Metropolitan police.
- The Act divided London into seventeen districts, each with its own police division, consisting of four inspectors and 144 constables.
- The police were given a uniform of blue overcoats and top hats to make them look different from the army.
- The new police force concentrated on patrolling their 'beats' (areas), in the hope of deterring and catching criminals.

How police forces developed in Britain 1829–1900

Developments in the 1830s

At first, the rest of Britain was slow to follow the example of the Metropolitan Police. This was due to a number of reasons:

- concerns over cost
- lack of co-operation between different areas
- central government did not force local areas to change; it was left optional.

Two new laws in the 1830s (the 1835 Municipal Corporations Act and the 1839 Rural Constabulary Act) tried to encourage towns and rural areas to set up their own police forces, but were only partly successful.

1842 – Creation of Scotland Yard

- The Metropolitan Police establish a dedicated detective unit.
- Detectives do not wear uniforms or patrol the beat, but instead wear ordinary 'plain clothes' and use intelligence to investigate and solve crimes.

The 1856 Police Act

- In 1856 the government passed the Police Act, which required all areas to set up a professional police force that would be centrally controlled.
- Police forces were to be inspected by the government to ensure they were delivering effective policing.
- The police aimed to prevent crime by actively looking for criminals. Criminals would be deterred from crime by knowing the police were looking for them.

1869 – Creation of National Crime Records

- Police forces began using modern technology such as the telegraph to quickly share information on crimes and suspects.

1878 – Creation of CID

- In 1878, the Criminal Investigations Department (CID) was set up to focus on investigating crime. By 1883, it employed 800 detectives.
- The CID developed new methods of investigation: in the 1880s, it attempted to catch Jack the Ripper by analysing handwriting.
- In 1902, for the first time, they convicted a burglar by using fingerprint evidence left at the crime scene.

Change by 1900

- By 1900, every area of Britain had a professional police force.
- Police forces began to share intelligence to help to catch criminals.
- Dedicated detective teams at Scotland Yard and the CID were using the latest technology to catch criminals.

This was a significant change from earlier methods of law enforcement.

▶ Developments in police forces in the 19th century

Exam-style question, Section B

Explain one way in which policing was similar in Tudor England and the early 18th century. **4 marks**

Exam tip

This question tests knowledge and understanding of key features and similarities and differences. Remember to give one way that policing was the same and support this with information from both periods.

Summary

- Early 18th century law enforcement continued to use methods similar to those used in the 16th–17th centuries.
- The Bow Street Runners were established in 1748, marking an important development in policing.
- In 1829, England's first professional police force, the Metropolitan Police, was established in London.
- The 1856 Police Act meant that all areas had to have a professional police force that was centrally controlled by government.
- In 1878, the Criminal Investigations Department was set up.

Checkpoint

Strengthen

S1 List two ways in which policing at the start of the 18th century was similar to the 16th century.

S2 Describe the changes introduced by the following laws:
- 1829 Metropolitan Police Act
- 1856 Police Act.

Challenge

C1 Explain why the setting up of Scotland Yard and CID was an important change in policing.

C2 Give one reason why it took a long time for policing to change in this period.

How confident do you feel about your answers to these questions? Form a small group, discuss the answers, then rewrite improved answers in your group.

3.4 Case study: The separate system at Pentonville Prison

Learning outcomes

- Understand the ideas behind changes in the prison system.
- Know about the conditions experienced by prisoners at Pentonville Prison when it first opened.
- Understand why Pentonville Prison was changed during the 19th century.

Timeline
Development of prisons in the 19th century

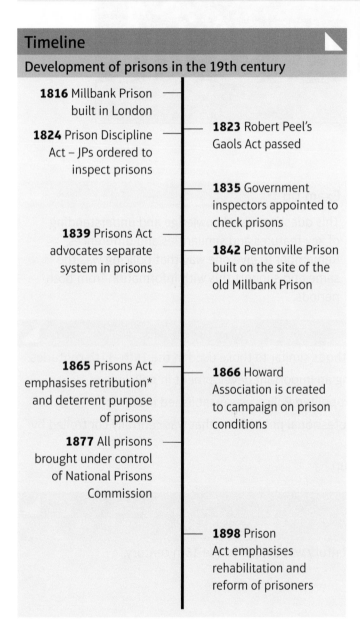

1816 Millbank Prison built in London

1824 Prison Discipline Act – JPs ordered to inspect prisons

1823 Robert Peel's Gaols Act passed

1835 Government inspectors appointed to check prisons

1839 Prisons Act advocates separate system in prisons

1842 Pentonville Prison built on the site of the old Millbank Prison

1865 Prisons Act emphasises retribution* and deterrent purpose of prisons

1866 Howard Association is created to campaign on prison conditions

1877 All prisons brought under control of National Prisons Commission

1898 Prison Act emphasises rehabilitation and reform of prisoners

The growth of the prison system in the mid 19th century

In the 18th century, prison was not generally used as a punishment in its own right; however, this began to change in the 19th century as concerns about rising crime grew and the private prison system came to an end.

The separate system at Pentonville Prison

Pentonville Prison was built in 1842 as a prototype* where the 'separate system' could be tested. Under this system, prisoners were kept apart as much as possible. They lived in separate cells and stayed there for up to 23 hours a day. Separate conditions were intended to:

- use solitude to make prisoners reflect upon their crime and try to improve themselves
- introduce them to religion
- stop them from being influenced by other criminals
- deter others from committing crime
- ensure retribution by making the prisoner 'pay' for their crime.

Key terms

Retribution*

A severe punishment, meant to match the severity of the crime.

Prototype*

A new idea or design that is tried out before more versions are made.

The building

The new prison was designed for the separate system, by keeping prisoners apart.

- The building was divided into five 'wings', with a base for staff in the centre.
- Each wing contained dozens of single cells in which prisoners would be kept in isolation.
- The cells were very small (4m × 2m) and contained a single small window, fixed with iron bars.
- The cells were heated and contained a small basin for washing and a basic toilet. This was to keep the prisoners healthy, but also so they didn't need to leave their cell.

Extend your knowledge

Joshua Jebb, Prison Surveyor General

Jebb was appointed Prison Surveyor General by the Home Office. He designed Pentonville as a 'model' prison in 1840–42. With a background in engineering, he designed the building to include modern features such as access to fresh air, heating and piped water. Between 1842 and 1877, 90 new prisons were built or extended using the design ideas that Jebb introduced at Pentonville.

Source A

Jebb's plans for the design of Pentonville Prison, 1842.

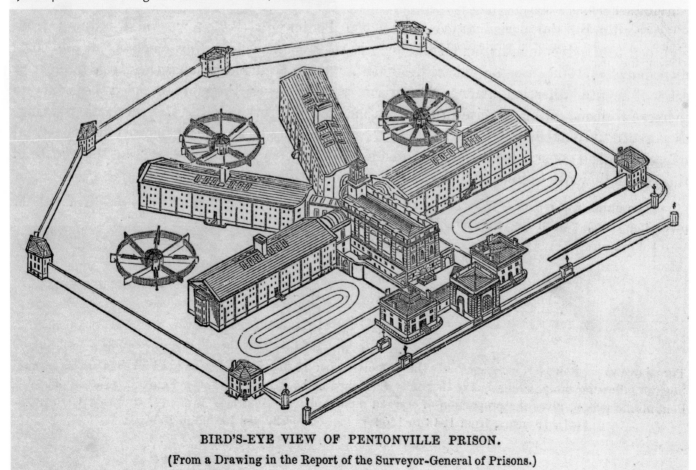

BIRD'S-EYE VIEW OF PENTONVILLE PRISON.
(From a Drawing in the Report of the Surveyor-General of Prisons.)

The living conditions

Discipline was harsh in Pentonville, and was designed to keep prisoners separate. Every feature of the prison was designed to add to their isolation:

- The building's walls were thick to stop prisoners communicating between cells.
- Prisoners worked in their cells so they remained isolated through the day. The work was deliberately very boring and repetitive: for example, oakum picking, which involved unravelling and cleaning old rope.
- Prisoners were allowed out for a short period of exercise or to go to chapel, but there were complicated systems in place to stop them from speaking to, or even seeing, one another. They wore face masks for exercise, and in chapel they sat alone wearing masks made of brown sacking.

The solitary conditions and lack of human contact meant many prisoners suffered from mental illness, including depression and psychosis*. There was also a high rate of suicide.

Key word

Psychosis*

A confused state where sufferers have hallucinations and delusions – seeing and imagining things that are not really there.

Source C

Prisoners at Pentonville during an outdoor exercise session. Face masks ensured that time outside their cells was still as isolated as possible.

Source B

Separate cell at Pentonville Prison 1842. The cell had a hammock-style bed and a mattress with a blanket. This cell had a weaving loom so the inmate could work without leaving the room.

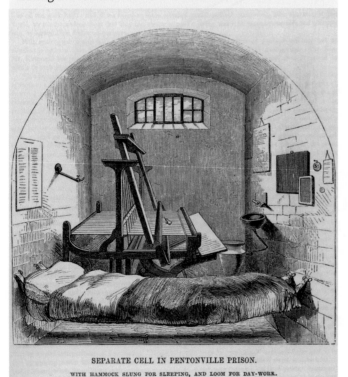

SEPARATE CELL IN PENTONVILLE PRISON.
WITH HAMMOCK SLUNG FOR SLEEPING, AND LOOM FOR DAY-WORK.

Activities ?

1. List three methods used by the authorities to keep Pentonville inmates separate from each other.
2. Suggest one reason why prisoners were made to do such boring and repetitive work.

Views of the separate system

Some reformers, like Elizabeth Fry, were worried about more prisons like Pentonville being built.

They wanted prisoners to have the chance to change their ways – to be rehabilitated.

However, many people in Government were more interesting in deterring and punishing criminals.

Elizabeth Fry wrote to government authorities about her concerns, including the Prison Surveyor General, Joshua Jebb.

Source D

From a letter written by Elizabeth Fry to Joshua Jebb, on the subject of Pentonville Prison, in 1841.

These cells appear to me calculated to excite such an awful terror in the mind... I am certain that separate confinement produces an unhealthy state, both of mind and body, and that, therefore everything should be done to counteract [balance] this influence... I consider light, air and the power of seeing something beyond the mere monotonous walls of a cell, highly important.

Activities ?

1 Read Source D. List two criticisms that Elizabeth Fry makes in her letter.

2 Write a letter from Joshua Jebb defending the 'separate system' in Pentonville Prison. Try to explain his justification for the conditions.

The late 19th century: increasingly harsh treatment of prisoners

In 1865, a Prisons Act was passed which made conditions in prisons even harsher. It did not aim to reform prisoners through religious faith or hard work.

The Assistant Director of Prisons, Sir Edmund Du Cane, declared that prisoners would get 'Hard labour, hard fare and hard board'. This meant:

- hard labour: physically demanding work for up to 12 hours every day
- hard fare: a deliberately boring and bland diet, with the same food served on the same day every week
- hard board: wooden board beds instead of the hammocks prisoners had slept on previously.

Source E

The writer Oscar Wilde was held in Pentonville Prison in 1898. This is an extract from a letter he wrote to the *Daily Chronicle* newspaper, urging reforms of the system.

Deprived of books, of all human intercourse [conversation], isolated from every humane and humanising influence, condemned to eternal silence... treated like an unintelligent animal... the wretched man who is confined in an English prison can hardly escape becoming insane.

Summary

- Pentonville was a prototype prison which aimed to keep prisoners as separate as possible.
- The government was concerned with punishing wrongdoing and deterring others from crime by ensuring conditions were sufficiently harsh.
- The conditions became even harsher with the 1865 Prisons Act, which aimed to enforce a strict, uniform system of punishment.

Checkpoint

Strengthen

S1 Give two reasons why prisoners were likely to develop mental illness under the seperate system.

S2 Why were inmates forced to do work like oakum picking?

S3 What was the purpose of making convicts do hard labour like climbing the treadwheel?

Challenge

C1 Do you think that hard labour would have made a prisoner change their behaviour after they were released from prison?

C2 Describe the impact of the 1865 Prisons Act.

How confident do you feel about your answers to these questions? If you're not sure you answered them well, discuss the answers with a partner and record your conclusions. Your teacher can give you some hints.

Name: Robert Peel

Key roles: Home Secretary (1822–27, 1828–30), Prime Minister (1834–35, 1841–46)

Key achievements:
- Seen as the 'father of modern policing' for setting up the Metropolitan Police force in 1829, which became the model for other police forces across the country.
- Trying to reform prisons with the 1823 Gaols Act.

What made him an effective reformer?
- Peel listened to others and took on board their suggestions, such as Elizabeth Fry's ideas for prison reform.
- Peel helped to guide new laws through parliament and persuaded other MPs to support them.
- He used his positions of power to bring about change.

Peel's penal* reforms in the 1820s

Peel was responsible for some significant penal reforms in the 1820s.

Changes to the penal code

Peel listened to reformers such as Elizabeth Fry and tried to make punishment fairer and more logical.

- Peel reduced the number of crimes punishable by death to 100.
- Minor crimes were punished more proportionately*.

Prison reform

Peel persuaded parliament to pass the 1823 Gaols Act. This said that:

- Prisoners should receive regular visits from prison chaplains*.
- Jailers should be paid so they had no need to make money from prisoners.
- Female prisoners should be watched over by female warders.
- Prisoners were not to be held in chains or irons.

However, the Act led to only limited change as there were no paid inspectors to put the new law into practice until the 1853 Prison Act.

Key terms

Penal*
Involving punishment.

Proportionately*
In a fair and balanced way. A proportionate punishment would be harsher for a serious crime and less harsh for a minor crime.

Chaplain*
A clergyman who works in an institution, e.g. a prison.

Timeline

Peel's penal code reforms, 1822–27

- **1822** Last hanging for shoplifting
- **1823** Gaols Act
- **1825** Capital crimes reduced by 100
- **1827** Black Act repealed

Metropolitan Police Force formed, 1829

Peel is most famous for founding the Metropolitan Police (see page 89).

Before 1829, each parish was responsible for their own law enforcement, and the standard differed widely across the capital. He wanted a system that would ensure similar standards of policing were provided all across London. Some wealthy London parishes had good numbers of trained watchmen, while some poorer areas had very inadequate policing.

The first Metropolitan Police officers were appointed in September 1829.

What did the job involve?

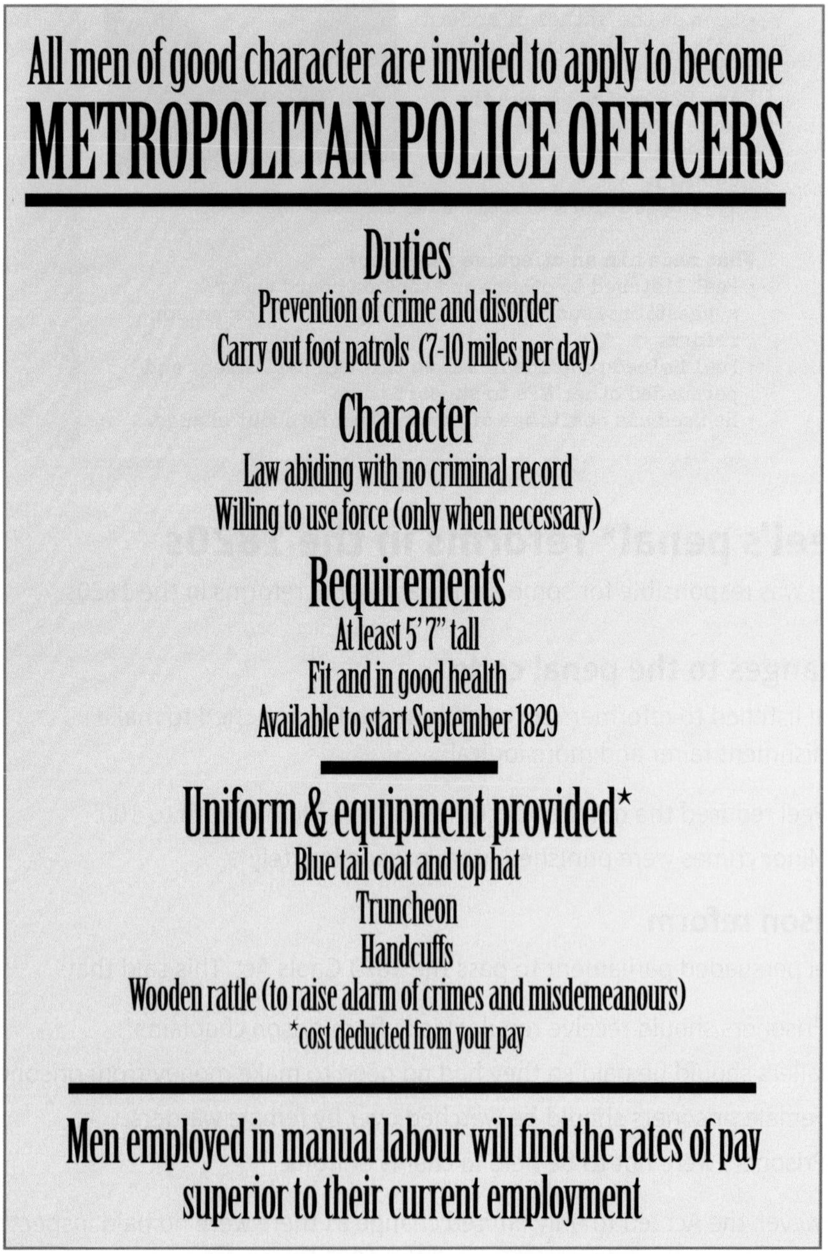
All men of good character are invited to apply to become
METROPOLITAN POLICE OFFICERS
Duties
Prevention of crime and disorder
Carry out foot patrols (7-10 miles per day)
Character
Law abiding with no criminal record
Willing to use force (only when necessary)
Requirements
At least 5' 7" tall
Fit and in good health
Available to start September 1829
Uniform & equipment provided*
Blue tail coat and top hat
Truncheon
Handcuffs
Wooden rattle (to raise alarm of crimes and misdemeanours)
*cost deducted from your pay
Men employed in manual labour will find the rates of pay superior to their current employment

Figure 3.4 A job description for the new role of Metropolitan Police officer.

Extend your knowledge

Policing the City of London

Although Peel created the Metropolitan Police, the 'square mile' of the City of London refused to become part of it as they wanted to protect their historical independence. Even in the 21st century, the City of London has its own, independent police.

Source A

From a letter sent by Home Secretary Robert Peel to the new police commissioners in July 1829.

Hierarchy and pay structure

Superintendents – A yearly Salary of £200 each.

Inspectors – A yearly Salary of £100 each.

Sergeants – A daily pay of three shillings and sixpence each.

Police Constables – A daily pay of three shillings each.

The pay of the Sergeants and Constables will be subject to certain deductions, which may be hereafter directed.

I am Gentlemen, your most obedient humble Servant,

Robert Peel

Activities ?

1   Using the table below, and information from this section, write a list summarising new features of the Metropolitan Police compared with the old night watch system.

2   Describe one similarity between the night watch and the police.

Night watch	Police
• Responsible for lighting lamps in the street • Help with various public services like administering street cleaning • Expected to call out the time • Tasked with watching out for fires and raising the alarm • Prevent crime by patrolling the streets • Expected to capture criminals caught in the act	• Organised in a military-style hierarchy • Employed full-time with weekly pay funded through increased public taxation • Centrally organised, under one clear authority for London, answerable to the Home Secretary • Headquarters set up at Scotland Yard • Standardised training for all officers • 2,000 new recruits

Criticisms of the new police force

The new police officers faced a hostile reaction from the public and the press, for some of the following reasons:

• Cartoons portrayed them as poorly trained and from semi-criminal backgrounds.

• It was feared they would be used by the state to cut down on individual liberties.

• People worried that they would be like the French police, who were known for being heavy-handed.

• Some were concerned about the cost to the taxpayer.

Source B

Letter of complaint about a London policeman's conduct, written in April 1830.

Gentlemen,

We are all so deeply interested in the good management and efficiency of the New Police, that I feel myself reluctantly bound to inform you of the misconduct of the Superintendent in this division of Brixton by being on duty on Tuesday night in a state of intoxication [drunk].

Source C

A cartoon, titled '*Reviewing the blue devils, alias the raw lobsters, alias the bludgeon men*', published in 1833. It illustrates some common criticisms of police recruits. Some of the captions read:

By Jasus, I vish your honor would give us a few throats to cut for we have had enough of breaking heads.

We'll do anything for money.

I vish I vos in the Vork-House (workhouse) once more vere they took me from.

I wish I was sweeping the crossing again.

REVIEWING THE BLUE DEVILS, ALIAS THE RAW LOBSTERS, ALIAS THE BLUDGEON MEN.

Activities

1 Discuss Source C in pairs. What impression do you get of Victorian policemen from this source?

2 Using you knowledge, explain why you think the author might have had a low opinion of policemen at that time.

Peel's attempts to reduce opposition to the police

Peel and his police commissioners understood the public concern about the introduction of the Metropolitan Police. The commissioners drew up and issued clear guidelines to all new police recruits. The principles included the following, which still provide the foundations for modern policing in Britain today.

Activities ?

1 Match the following statements to Peel's nine principles in Figure 3.5.

   a Effective policing is judged by the absence of crime

   b Force is the last resort of a police officer

   c Police should not overstep their authority

   d Police are citizens in uniform

   e Police should be role models representing the public

   f Policing has to be by consent of the public not the government

   g Policing must focus on maintaining law and order

   h Police must be objective and professional

   i Police need to encourage public co-operation to be effective

2 Which of these principles would have been most reassuring to those who criticised the new police force?

3 Which of these principles would have been the most difficult to achieve?

1. The basic mission for which the police exist is to prevent crime and disorder.

2. The ability of the police to perform their duties is dependent upon public approval of police actions.

3. Police must secure the willing co-operation of the public to be able to secure and maintain respect of the public.

4. The more physical force we use, the less the public will co-operate.

5. The police must stick to the law instead of public opinion.

6. Police use physical force when it is necessary to enforce the law or to restore order, but should only do so if persuasions and warnings have failed.

7. The police should remember that the police are the public and the public are the police. The police are only members of the public who are paid to enforce the law.

8. The police should always direct their action towards police work, and should not try to replace the courts.

9. The test of police efficiency is the absence of crime and disorder.

Figure 3.5 A summary of advice given to new Metropolitan Police recruits.

Was Peel a 'great reformer'?

Historians have different ideas about why Peel wanted penal reforms. Some argue he partly wanted to make prison more humane, while others argue he wanted to set up a more effective system for punishing criminals. Interpretations 1 and 2 highlight these different views, and the arguments about the impact of his reforms.

Interpretation 1

From *Sir Robert Peel: the Life and Legacy* by Richard Gaunt, published in 2010.

Peel's criminal law reforms were not designed to result in less punishment but in its more precise and efficient application. It follows from this that there would be no immediate down-turn in capital executions... He may not have been a 'great hangman', but nor was he 'a great reformer'.

Interpretation 2

From *Victorian England, Portrait of an Age* by G.M. Young, published in 1936.

His frigid efficiency covered an almost passionate concern for the welfare of the people.

THINKING HISTORICALLY Change and continuity (4a)

Significance

Look at Interpretation 1 and Interpretation 2 above.

1   What does Gaunt believe was the purpose of Peel's reforms?

2   What does Young argue was the purpose of Peel's reforms?

3   Sum up the difference between the two interpretations, using a quote from each.

Summary

- Robert Peel held a number of ministerial roles and became Home Secretary in 1822.
- During the 1820s, he brought in wide-ranging changes to criminal law and prison reforms.
- He had some sympathy with the arguments of 19th-century reformers, and also wanted to use the law more effectively and introduce a new penal code.
- In 1829, he introduced the first professional police force, which initially faced a hostile attitude from the public and the media.

Checkpoint

Strengthen

S1 Name two criticisms that people made about Peel's police force.

S2 Describe the uniform and equipment issued to the first Metropolitan Police officers.

S3 Write out two of Peel's policing principles (from Figure 3.5) and then explain what they mean in your own words.

Challenge

C1 Describe two differences between the work of a Metropolitan Police officer and a night watchman.

C2 Write a short paragraph explaining why Peel is important to the history of crime and punishment.

How confident are you about your answers to these questions? Reread this section, then try answering them again.

Recap: c1700–c1900: Crime, punishment and law enforcement in the 18th and 19th centuries

Recall quiz

1. What law was broken by the Tolpuddle martyrs?
2. What date did transportation to Australia begin?
3. What book was published by John Howard?
4. Which prison did Elizabeth Fry help to reform for women?
5. Define the term 'treadwheel'.
6. When was the police service brought under the control of national government?
7. Who started the Bow Street Runners?
8. What government position was held by Robert Peel before he became Prime Minister?
9. Which city was policed by the Metropolitan Police Force?
10. Name two famous highwaymen.

Activity

Matching pairs

Use pairs of A5 file cards, or pieces of A4 paper cut into two. On each card/piece of paper, write a name or topic from below, on the other add brief revision notes. Make more cards on other topics from this chapter. You could use different colours of paper or ink for the different categories: e.g. reformers, places.

Turn all the cards face down and turn them face up two at a time. Collect matching pairs, e.g. Robert Peel and the notes you made about his role. If you are playing with other people, as you take a pair, explain the details to the others.

Reformers	Places	Technology	Beginnings	Politicians and officials	Endings
John Howard	Bow Street	Fingerprinting	Metropolitan Police Act, 1829	Robert Peel	Abolition of public execution, 1868
Elizabeth Fry	Scotland Yard	Telegraph communication	Gaols Act, 1823	Joshua Jebb	End of transportation, 1868
Edmund Du Cane	Australia	Pentonville Prison	CID, 1877	Henry Fielding	Repeal of Black Act, 1814

Writing historically: using phrases to build detail

The best historical writing uses carefully structured phrases to incorporate facts.

Learning outcomes

By the end of this lesson, you will understand how to:

- add facts to your writing
- express your ideas in more detail.

Definitions

Adjective: a word that provides additional information about a noun, e.g. 'clear, precise writing'.

Preposition: a word giving information about position or time, e.g. '**in** the 19th century', '**during** the war', '**after** several years'.

How can I add factual detail to my writing?

Prepositions show the connections between other words or phrases in a sentence. They include words like:

in	at	on	after	before	during	with	without	from	to	between

Prepositions can be used to add important information about the time and/or place that significant events took place in. For example:

During the Civil War...	In the early 1800s...	Before Peel's reforms...
With the building of the turnpikes...	Without this knowledge...	From the beginning of this period...

1. Look at the response to this exam-style question. Rewrite the response, adding more information using prepositions. The highlighted sections show where the answer needs more information – usually, **when** or **where** these events happened.

> The role of reformers was the main reason why prison conditions improved in the 19th and 20th centuries. How far do you agree? **(20 marks)**

Prisons were of a very poor standard and the conditions were dirty and terrible for the prisoners' health. Some reformers argued that prisons had to be improved. Elizabeth Fry visited Newgate prison. Once conditions were known, the public and politicians were more willing to make improvements. The breakthrough came when the first 'model prisons', like Pentonville were developed. Others followed, but all were dependent on the ideas of reformers that prisoners should be reformed not just punished.

The government's role became more significant. The introduction of prison inspections improved the standards.

How can I add detail to my writing?

One way in which you can add more information to your answer is by adding **adjectives** and **prepositions**.

Compare these two versions of a sentence:

> The work of reformers gave people access to better prisons. Without their new ideas criminals would have remained in bad conditions and politicians' opinions would not have changed.

> The work of reformers gave convicts, especially women and children, access to better prison conditions. Without their work, like publishing research on the unhealthy conditions for inmates, the focus on reform would not have come about for vulnerable prisoners like the young and ill. Furthermore, politicians like Peel would not have been so aware of the problems.

Look at the copy of the second version below. The adjectives and prepositions have been highlighted.

> The work of reformers gave convicts especially women and children access to better prison conditions. Without their work, like publishing research on the unhealthy conditions for inmates, the focus on reform would not have come about for vulnerable prisoners like the young and ill. Furthermore, politicians like Peel would not have been so aware of the problems.

2. What kind of information and detail can adjectives and prepositions add to historical writing?

Improving an answer

3. Now look at the next section of this response below. How could you use prepositions and adjectives to make the response more precise and detailed? Use your own ideas or look at the comments for help.

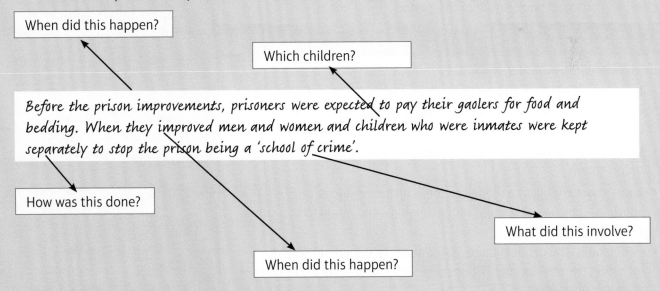

When did this happen?

Which children?

Before the prison improvements, prisoners were expected to pay their gaolers for food and bedding. When they improved men and women and children who were inmates were kept separately to stop the prison being a 'school of crime'.

How was this done?

What did this involve?

When did this happen?

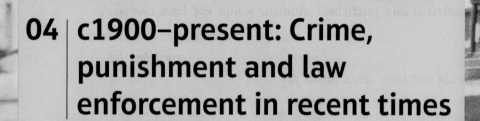

04 | c1900–present: Crime, punishment and law enforcement in recent times

In the 20th century, the changes in society had a big effect on crime, punishment and law enforcement. The role of the state in ordinary people's lives also increased, largely as a result of the First and Second World Wars. Social attitudes changed dramatically during the 20th century, which led to some activities being decriminalised. Other activities became illegal for the first time, creating new crimes.

Crime detection and prevention during this period changed significantly as a result of developments in science and technology. New communications technologies, in particular, have had an important impact on the types of crime carried out and on crime detection.

Changing attitudes about the rehabilitation and welfare of offenders has also been an important feature of this period.

Learning outcomes

By the end of this chapter you will:

- be able to describe continuity and change in the nature of crimes, and changing definitions of crime – including driving offences, race crimes and drug crimes

- understand the role of the authorities and local communities in law enforcement

- know about changes to the police force, including: increasing specialisation, use of science and technology, and emphasis on crime prevention

- understand why major changes came about in the prison system, including the development of open prisons and specialised treatment of young offenders

- know about the treatment of conscientious objectors in the First and Second World Wars

- know about the abolition of the death penalty in Britain, and understand the significance of the Derek Bentley case.

4.1 Crime and definitions of crime, c1900–present

Changing social attitudes have caused changes in the law in every era, but this is particularly true of the 20th century – especially the 1960s. The 1960s was a decade when there were many changes in social attitudes; many activities that had been crimes were decriminalised, while some activities became crimes.

Key terms

Homophobic*

Prejudiced against people who are gay.

Hate crime*

A crime motivated by prejudice against the victim's race, gender, disability or sexual orientation.

Timeline

Changing definitions of crime in the 20th century

1967 Sexual Offences Act

1968 Abortion Act passed
Race Relations Act passed

1976 Domestic Violence Act

1991 Law recognises rape within marriage as a crime

2000 Terrorism Act

2005 Criminal Justice Act raises severity of 'hate crimes'

2006 Racial and Religious Hatred Act

2015 Modern Slavery Act

Changing definitions of crime

Homophobic crime

- Before 1967, homosexuality was illegal in the UK.
- If a person was attacked for being gay in a homophobic* attack, this was treated the same as any other crime.

Changes

- Changing attitudes in the 1960s led to the passing of the 1967 Sexual Offences Act, which decriminalised homosexuality for men aged over 21.
- Attitudes continued to change, and in 2005 the Criminal Justice Act classified homophobic attacks as a hate crime*, which were treated more seriously by the authorities.

Outcome

- Homosexuality is no longer a crime.
- Homophobic attacks become a new crime.

Race Crime

- From the 1940s onwards, many people moved to Britain from former colonies of the British Empire, meaning Britain became much more multicultural.
- Many immigrants experienced discrimination, however racism was not illegal.

Changes

- In 1968 the Race Relations Act led to a new definition of crime, as it became illegal to discriminate against someone because of their race, background or country of origin.
- In 2006, the law was extended to define spreading racial or religious hatred as a crime.

Outcome

- Racial and religious discrimination becomes a new crime.

Domestic Violence

- Before the 20th century, the common view in society was that men were the dominant partners in relationships, and women were expected to obey. In general, the authorities saw violence and abuse in relationships as a private matter and did not intervene. Even rape within marriage was not a crime.
- During the 20th century attitudes changed, as women campaigned for and gained the vote and took important roles in the First and Second World Wars. In the 1960s women campaigned for equal rights for women, which helped to change attitudes further. Society increasingly started to stand up for the rights of women.

Changes

- In 1976 the Domestic Violence Act was passed, which gave women the right to ask for an injunction* against a violent partner.
- In 1991, the law was changed and it became possible to prosecute a husband for raping his wife.
- In 2014, the law changed to make controlling and coercive behaviour (using force or threats) towards a partner a crime. This could include: telling a partner who they can see, what they can wear, stopping access to money, controlling their access to a phone, and controlling when they can leave the home.

Outcome

- Rape, abuse and controlling behaviour within a marriage becomes a crime.

Abortion

- Until 1967 it was illegal to terminate a pregnancy, unless it was thought the mother could die as a result of the pregnancy.
- Many women had 'backstreet abortions' carried out by someone without medical training. Some women also tried to end their pregnancies themselves using coat hangers and poison. As a result, many women died.

Changes

- By the 1960s, attitudes began to change and many people demanded a change in the law.
- In 1967 the Abortion Act legalised abortion if the child was likely to have serious disabilities, or if the mother was at risk.
- In 1968, the legal limit for abortion was 28 weeks, however this has reduced over time.

Outcome

- Abortion is no longer a crime.

Attitudes towards social crimes

'Social crimes' are crimes that many people in society accept to some degree. Examples include:

- tax evasion
- using illegal drugs
- copyright theft
- minor driving offences.

Smuggling and poaching are examples of social crimes which have existed for many years.

Source A

The entertainment industry campaigns to make illegal sales of copyright material socially unacceptable.

Most people in society would agree that smuggling drugs worth millions of pounds is wrong, and would support stopping drug traffickers. However, fewer people worry about smuggling laws when buying tax-free cigarettes or alcohol that has been smuggled.

Another good example is copyright. Lots of people download music, games and films from the internet although they are subject to copyright laws (see page 111). Because they are widely and freely available on the internet, most people do not view this behaviour as criminal. It is difficult to enforce laws when they are not supported by society, because often offenders are not reported.

Driving offences

Sometimes, society's attitudes about the seriousness of a crime can change dramatically over time. Drink driving and speeding are both good examples of this.

- 1925 – it became illegal to drive a car while drunk.
- 1967 – a new law set a maximum limit for the amount of alcohol a person could have in their bloodstream and legally drive.
- Since the 1970s, government campaigns have made drink-driving and speeding much more socially unacceptable, and they are now generally condemned by the public.

Drug-taking

Many drugs first became illegal in 1971 when the Misuse of Drugs Act was passed. The legalisation of some classes of drugs is a controversial issue in society.

- Some people argue that taking a drug should be a personal choice as long as it does not harm others.
- Others argue legalisation is needed to help tackle crimes associated with illegal drug-dealing, including sex trafficking and gang-related violence.

New opportunities for old crimes

Some crimes may appear to be new, but are actually older crimes that are carried out in different ways.

Terrorism

Terrorism is not a new crime.

Terrorism can be defined as using violence, fear and intimidation to make people aware of a political issue. The Gunpowder Plot could be described as terrorism.

In the 1970s and 1980s, the IRA (Irish Republican Army) used terrorist tactics to campaign for political independence from the rest of the UK.

In recent years, attention has switched to Al-Qaeda and Isis, who have been responsible for acts of terror in Europe, such as the attack seen in Source B. There are also many other terrorist threats, such as from far-right* movements which has led to attacks like the murder of MP Jo Cox in June 2016 by far-right supporter Thomas Mair.

Modern-day terrorists use the internet to communicate and spread their message. The methods have changed since the Gunpowder plot but the crime is the same.

Key term

Far-right*

Political groups, like fascism, on the extreme right of politics who often hold beliefs considered to be racist, sexist and undemocratic.

Source B

The aftermath of a terrorist attack on a London bus, 7 July 2005.

Source C

From a newspaper report about the July 2005 terrorist attacks, which appeared in the *Daily Telegraph*.

Jonathan Evans, the director-general of MI5 who has only been in the job a fortnight, said: "My service has never been complacent. The attack on 7 July in London was a terrible event. The sense of disappointment, felt across the service, at not being able to prevent the attack (despite our efforts to prevent all such atrocities) will always be with us.

"The reality is that, whilst we will continue to do everything in our power to protect the UK public, we must be honest about what can and cannot be prevented in a democratic society that values its freedoms."

Activity ?

Hold a class discussion on this question: 'Why do law enforcers find it so hard to prevent terrorist attacks?'

People-trafficking

This involves people from poorer countries being brought to the UK and being forced to work for very low wages, or no wages at all. Some women and children are forced into prostitution. Often criminal gangs control these people through intimidation and imprisonment.

People-trafficking is not a new crime. In the 19th century poor girls were sold into prostitution. In the 1830s, the term 'white slave trade' was used to describe the victims of this crime.

Key term

Blackmail*

To threaten someone by releasing embarrassing or confidential information if they do not pay a sum of money.

Cybercrime
The internet has enabled criminals to conduct old crimes, such as fraud, on a much bigger scale.

Fraud
Fraud means impersonating someone else to make money illegally.

- In the past, this may have been done in person – for example, asking people to donate to a fake charity.
- Today, criminals use methods like e-mail to try and trick people into revealing their bank details. It is a growing problem as banking moves online.

Copyright theft
Copyright laws provide artists and companies with the right to be paid for their work, and it applies to books, music, films and games. It is illegal to make copies of these without permission.

- In the late 20th century, copyright theft became an issue when people began recording music and film onto video and cassette tapes.
- In the 21st century, the internet has made the problem bigger, as it allows people to copy and share media through illegal downloads.

Extortion
Extortion involves forcing someone to pay money by using threats or blackmail*.

- In the past, extortion was carried out in person, or via letters or on the telephone.
- Now, criminals might threaten to hack a business's computer system unless they agree to pay.

▶ New ways of committing old crimes

Exam-style question, Section B ●

'Types of crimes have not changed since the beginning of the 19th century, only the methods used to commit them.'

How far do you agree? Explain your answer. You may use the following in your answer:

- fraud
- race crimes.

You **must** also use information of your own. **16 marks**

Exam tip ●

To answer this question, plan your answer by making a table with two columns. On one side, try to give examples of types of crimes that have remained similar since 1800, but may be committed in new ways – such as fraud. On the other, try to think of examples of new crimes – for example, race crimes.

Summary ◥

- Changing social attitudes have led to things that were previously legal being redefined as crimes.
- The 1968 Race Relations Act made it illegal to refuse jobs, housing or public services to anyone on the basis of their race, ethnic background or country of origin.
- During the 20th century there were significant changes to the laws on abuse between people in a relationship.
- New technology and changing social attitudes have changed how driving offences are viewed and tackled.
- Digital technology has enabled criminals to carry out many old crimes in new ways.

Checkpoint ◥

Strengthen

S1 What is a 'hate crime'?

S2 Give two examples of cybercrime.

S3 Write a definition for the term 'terrorism'.

Challenge

C1 Give one example of an activity that has become decriminalised due to changing social attitudes.

C2 What examples of 'social crimes' can you think of after 1900?

How confident do you feel about your answers to these questions? Reread the section and then try answering the questions again. If you're still not sure, discuss them with your teacher.

4.2 Law enforcement, c1900–present

Developments in policing since 1900

In 1900, every area across Britain had its own police force. The 200 separate forces had no central records on crime or criminals, and rarely shared information or worked together.

For individual police officers, the majority of the working day was spent patrolling the local area – 'walking the beat'. They travelled on foot and used a whistle to call for assistance or raise the alarm.

During the 20th century, policing changed in many ways.

- Women were first recruited to join the police force in the 1920s.
- In 1947, the Police Training College was set up to improve the training of police officers, who previously learned on the job.
- Other important developments included:
  - increased use of science and technology
  - more specialised departments and roles for police officers
  - a move towards more crime prevention.

All these changes increased the cost of policing, which is now far higher than it was at the beginning of the 20th century.

Modern policing makes increasing use of new technology to solve and prevent crime. New technologies can make police work quicker and more reliable.

Science and technology

1900s
In 1901, Fingerprint Branch is set up at the Metropolitan Police headquarters at New Scotland Yard. The National Fingerprint System keeps a record of fingerprints from everyone arrested, creating a database which all forces can use to identify criminals.

The fact that there are different blood types is discovered in 1901. Police can use blood samples from crime scenes to identify criminals.

Improved microscopes make it possible to find smaller quantities of blood at crime scenes to use as evidence.

Photography is used to record crime scenes.

In 1909, police bicycles are introduced, allowing officers to pursue criminals more quickly.

1930s
Police cars are now quite common. Two-way radios are installed in cars for better communication with the station and other officers.

999 emergency telephone number is introduced.

1960s
The Metropolitan Police first uses computers to process payroll and pensions.

1980
The Police National Computer is launched, capable of holding the records of 25 million individuals.

1988
First murder convictions based on DNA samples from the victims and the accused. DNA can be identified in tiny quantities of hair, skin or body fluids.

1995
National Automatic Fingerprint Identification System and National DNA Database set up to share information that can be used to identify criminals.

Figure 4.1 Technological milestones in policing in the 20th century.

Source A

A photograph of a 1950s police phone box, which was used to report crimes and ask for back-up.

Activities

1. Look at the table. Find three examples of 21st century technology cutting down on the number of police needed to investigate crime, compared to the 1900s.

2. How could these technologies impact on individual freedoms? Make notes of your ideas, then discuss them in a small group.

Preventing crime	Solving crime
Breathalysers and speed cameras Breathalysers were introduced in 1967 and let traffic police test drivers' blood alcohol level at the roadside. Speed cameras were introduced in 1992. These make it possible to catch more people drink-driving and speeding, and act as a deterrent.	**Improved communications** Recording and sharing information directly at a crime scene, using digital technologies like tablets and smartphones.
Closed circuit television (CCTV) People are less likely to commit crime if they know they are being filmed.	**Forensic science** Forensic teams carry out highly detailed searches at crime scenes, looking for evidence such as DNA, fingerprints and objects left by criminals. DNA and fingerprint samples can be matched to criminals' records in the national databases.
Mass video surveillance Computer software allows private companies to analyse large amounts of footage and anticipate acts of terrorism and other crimes.	**Data management** These are used to store and share information about crime, e.g. the National DNA Database held records of 5.7 million individuals' DNA profiles in 2015.
Biometric screening This uses unique body characteristics, such as fingerprints or eye patterns, to restrict access to data, places and buildings.	**Improved computer software** New software can rapidly analyse video data to identify criminals. This would have taken far longer when a police officer had to watch the video in real time.

Source B

Source B

Police forensics team searching a crime scene.

Increasing specialisation of police roles since 1900

During the 20th century, police forces developed many specialist departments and units to help detectives tackle specific types of crime. They are often set up in response to new types of crime.

- For example, the Metropolitan Police Bomb Squad was set up in 1971 when there was an increasing number of terrorist attacks by the IRA and other groups.
- A more recent example is the National Hi-tech Crime Unit, set up in 2001 to deal with online crimes, including hacking, credit card fraud and virus attacks.

Fraud Squad

The first specialist Fraud Squad was set up in London, in 1946, to tackle crime in business and the stock market. These crimes required police officers with expert knowledge of finance and business to investigate them. The Fraud Squad also tackles other high-value crimes like art theft. Today the Fraud Squad is increasingly involved in investigating cyber crime.

Specialist drug-trade units

In 1971, the Misuse of Drugs Act was passed. This made the use of various substances – including heroin, cocaine and cannabis – criminal offences. Drug crime is policed by special operations units that tackle drug crimes by:

- disrupting criminal activity and organisations
- monitoring known drug users
- preventing the further spread of drug use.

The National Crime Agency, set up in 2013, uses intelligence and data on known criminal groups to predict and stop drug hauls reaching the country from abroad, and to disrupt supply networks for drugs manufactured within the UK.

All local police forces have special squads to deal with drug dealers in their areas. These squads try to disrupt the trade with raids on buildings where dealers store and supply drugs.

Source C

Part of a seizure of heroin smuggled into the UK.

115

Dog handling units

The first specially trained police dogs were used by police officers in south London, in 1938, as they patrolled their local beat. A specialist dog section was set up within the Metropolitan Police in 1946. By the 1950s, most police forces had dog units.

Today dogs are trained to:

- sniff out drugs
- find explosives
- track and catch criminals
- search for missing persons
- strengthen the police presence at major events.

Special Branch

Every police force has its own Special Branch to tackle threats to national security and terrorism. They work with MI5, the security service, to detect and prevent terrorist attacks. Using surveillance*, they try to intercept possible terrorist acts and warn local police of threats.

Crime prevention

In the 21st century, police forces have increasingly focused on preventing crime. This type of policing can involve:

- working with schools to help young people avoid crime
- giving people advice on how to protect their homes
- predicting where crime might occur to help plan how to prevent it
- the use of Police Community Support Officers* to reduce anti-social behaviour and the fear of crime.

Key terms

Surveillance*

To monitor the behaviour of criminals using CCTV and by tracking their phone and computer activity.

Police Community Support Officer (PCSO)*

Work with police officers and have some, but not all, of their responsibilities.

Neighbourhood Watch

Origins of Neighbourhood Watch

During the 1980s the prime minister, Margaret Thatcher, led a Conservative government that wanted to make people feel like they had more control over their own safety and to encourage Active Citizenship*. Thatcher's new system would be run by volunteers.

Neighbourhood Watch came from the US. It was originally set up in Chicago and was believed to be successful in tackling crime.

Britain in the early 1980s saw a dramatic increase in crimes and society was keen to find new ways to reduce it.

Aims of Neighbourhood Watch

In 1982, the UK's first Neighbourhood Watch scheme was set up to try to prevent crime. The scheme encourages neighbours to keep an eye on each others' property.

Aims include:

- helping the police prevent crime, by encouraging local vigilance*
- reducing fear of crime, by increasing community involvement
- reporting crime trends to the police.

In the early 1980s, the number of local Neighbourhood Watches rose from 1,000 to 29,000.

Key terms

Active Citizenship*
People taking an active role in their community in order to improve it.

Vigilance*
Keeping a careful watch for danger or possible criminal activity.

Vigilante*
A person who takes the law into their own hands. Vigilantes often operate in groups.

Source E

Sign showing that residents in this area take part in a Neighbourhood Watch scheme.

Source F

Bill Pitt MP, speaking about the Neighbourhood Watch scheme in a House of Commons debate on 28 February 1983.

Crime is growing and we are seen as losing the battle as Sir Kenneth Newman says... I welcome his suggestion that the community should play its part in conquering crime. I welcome the neighbourhood watch. I had strong reservations... because I wondered whether some people would set up vigilante* groups.

Source G

From the Police Commissioner, Sir Kenneth Newman's, Annual Report for 1986.

We have always sought public co-operation, but in the past we have relied largely on exhortation [sending encouraging messages]. Over the last four years, however, we have been deliberately organising a coherent structure within which the public will be enabled to work with us in a purposeful manner. The building blocks so far are consultative groups, neighbourhood watch schemes, business watch schemes, victim support schemes, crime prevention panels and estate policing projects. Neighbourhood Watch has increased the commitment of members to the quality of life in their neighbourhood.

Activities ?

1 What does Bill Pitt say, in Source F, about the reasons why Neighbourhood Watch was needed?

2 What concerns did Bill Pitt have about the impact of Neighbourhood Watch schemes?

3 Read Source G. According to the author, what changes did the schemes introduce?

Exam-style question, Section B

Explain one way that the system of community law enforcement in the 20th century was different from community law enforcement in the 16th century.

4 marks

Exam tip

This question tests knowledge and understanding of key features and difference. Remember to give one way community law enforcement in the 20th century was different from the 16th century system and then add details from both periods to show the difference.

Public attitudes towards Neighbourhood Watch schemes

Some people believed the scheme made a significant and positive change. Others claimed that the system was ineffective and did not prevent crime.

Figure 4.2 Some common views of the Neighbourhood Watch scheme in the 1980s.

Summary

- Important developments in modern policing include increased use of science and technology, and increasing co-operation at a national level.
- In the 20th century there was increasing specialisation in police forces, with special divisions set up and better training.
- There was an increasing emphasis on crime prevention, including voluntary Neighbourhood Watch schemes.

Checkpoint

Strengthen

S1 Describe two ways in which technology helps the police to solve or prevent crime in the 20th century.

S2 Describe the role of forensic investigators.

S3 Describe two ways in which the community has helped to prevent crime since the 1980s.

Challenge

C1 Explain the factors that led to the creation of Neighbourhood Watch in the 1980s.

How confident do you feel about your answers to these questions? Form a small group and discuss any questions you are not sure about. Look for the answers in this section. Now rewrite your answers as a group.

4.3 Changes in punishment, c1900–present

Abolition of the death penalty

From Anglo-Saxon Britain to the 20th century, execution was used as the ultimate punishment.

However, it was used less and less from the beginning of the 19th century, and by the 1830s murder and treason were the only crimes punished with the death penalty. Throughout the 19th century, politicians tried to introduce new laws to end the death penalty, but they were unsuccessful.

During the 20th century, attitudes began to change, until new laws abolished* the death penalty.

Key term

Abolished*

Banned or made illegal.

In the early 1950s, around 15 people a year were executed. However, the Homicide Act of 1957 stated the death penalty could only be used for the most serious cases of murder, known as capital murders (see Extend your knowledge on the next page). After 1957, there was an average of four executions per year.

In 1965, the Murder Act suspended the death penalty for murder for five years. This decision was made permanent in 1969. A few crimes still carried the death penalty, including:

- espionage (spying)
- arson (deliberate fire-starting) in the royal dockyards
- high treason
- piracy with violence.

The death penalty was not actually used for these crimes, and these were gradually added to the list of crimes not punished by death. The death penalty was ended for all crimes in 1998.

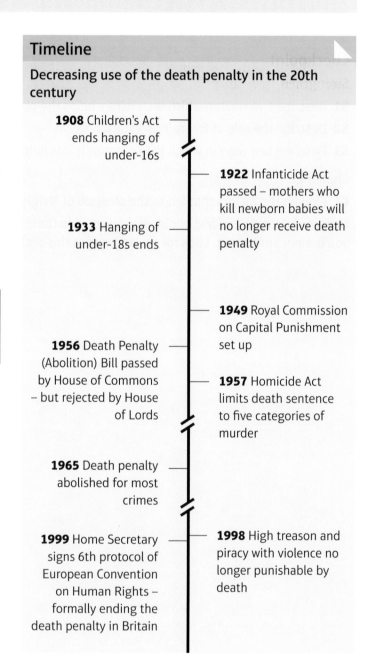

Timeline

Decreasing use of the death penalty in the 20th century

1908 Children's Act ends hanging of under-16s

1922 Infanticide Act passed – mothers who kill newborn babies will no longer receive death penalty

1933 Hanging of under-18s ends

1949 Royal Commission on Capital Punishment set up

1956 Death Penalty (Abolition) Bill passed by House of Commons – but rejected by House of Lords

1957 Homicide Act limits death sentence to five categories of murder

1965 Death penalty abolished for most crimes

1999 Home Secretary signs 6th protocol of European Convention on Human Rights – formally ending the death penalty in Britain

1998 High treason and piracy with violence no longer punishable by death

Source A

A newspaper headline announcing the abolition of capital punishment.

The role of government

In parliament, opinions about the death penalty were strongly divided. The House of Commons passed bills abolishing the death penalty in 1948 and 1956 – but these were blocked by the House of Lords.

The death penalty for most crimes was eventually abolished in 1965.

Changing attitudes

As the 20th century progressed, attitudes towards the death penalty changed.

This was part of a general change in society as most people became liberal* on a number of social issues.

Attitudes towards children

It was increasingly recognised that the law needed to treat children differently from adults. In 1908 the Children's Act said under-16s could no longer be sentenced to death.

Acts of Parliament (see timeline on page 124) raised the age of criminal responsibility* to eight, and then ten years old, while only those aged 18 or above could face the death penalty.

Changing attitudes to women

There was also an increased understanding that a women's mental health could be affected by pregnancy and childbirth.

The 1922 Infanticide Act ruled that women should not be punished with the death penalty if they killed a child shortly after birth.

Interpretation 1

From an article by Liz Homans, published in *History Today* in 2008.

At 8am on August 13th, 1964, Peter Allen and Gwynne Evans were hanged – Evans at Strangeways in Manchester, Allen at Walton Prison in Liverpool. They were the respective hangmen's last jobs. The following year Parliament voted to abolish the death penalty. This reform is often seen as emblematic [a symbol] of the 1960s, part of a shift towards a more 'permissive' [open and tolerant] society. However, the abolition of capital punishment did not reflect any sea change in public opinion, which remained firmly opposed to abolition. For abolitionists, the vote had nothing to do with any permissive society; it was the successful end of a long, long campaign.

Key terms

Miscarriage of justice*

When a court is thought to have made the wrong decision, e.g. convicting an innocent person.

Leniency*

To show mercy.

Controversial executions

In the 1950s, a series of controversial executions caused the public to question the death penalty more and more, and led to protests about the use of capital punishment. For more detail on the Derek Bentley trial, and its influence on the end of capital punishment, see Section 4.5.

1950	Timothy Evans	Hanged for murdering his wife and baby. Later evidence proved that they had been killed by a serial killer and Evans was innocent. There was a huge public outcry at this miscarriage of justice*.
1953	Derek Bentley	Hanged for the murder of a police officer. Bentley had learning difficulties and had not fired the gun himself but was prosecuted anyway.
1955	Ruth Ellis	Hanged for the murder of her violent and abusive boyfriend. He had attacked her when she was pregnant and caused her to miscarry. Ellis was also the mother of a young child who was orphaned by her mother's execution. A petition, with 50,000 signatures asking for leniency*, was ignored by the Home Secretary.

Source B

Crowds outside Holloway Prison, protesting against the execution of Ruth Ellis on 13 July 1955.

Activities

1 Explain why there was growing opposition to the death penalty in the 1950s, using at least one example from above.

2 Look at Interpretation 1. Does Homans believe that the death penalty was abolished because of more liberal attitudes in society, or because politicians were determined to abolish the death penalty **despite** public opinion?

Changes in the prison system

The use of prison as a punishment has increased since 1900. During the 20th century, ideas about what prison was for, and the type of treatment prisoners should expect, changed. The current cost of keeping a person in prison for a year is estimated at £40,000, and reoffending rates are very high. Questions are still being asked about the use of prison as a punishment in modern society.

Year	New idea	Practical outcomes
1896	Mentally ill prisoners treated separately to other prisoners.	Broadmoor Hospital opened.
1902	Hard labour ended.	No more treadwheels in prison.
1907	Alternatives to prisons used.	Probation* officers employed to check on offenders living outside prison.
1922	Increased focus on prisoner welfare.	Separate system of prisoners ended. New initiatives to improve conditions. Educational opportunities introduced.
1933	New focus on preparing prisoners for life after serving their sentence.	First open prison at New Hall, Wakefield. Open prisons offered a more relaxed regime. Prisoners were allowed out on day release to work and prepare for return into society.

Key term

Probation*

A period of good behaviour after release from prison. Former inmates are expected to regularly meet probation officers who supervise them.

Source C

Vicky Pryce describes her experience of East Sutton Park open prison in an article published on the *Daily Mail* website in October 2013.

It was a far cry from what we had left behind. Even so, I was astonished to discover that Friday night was karaoke night in the pool room between 8.30 and 10.30 – which I went to on my first night. Saturday night was bingo night, for which you had to pay a fee of 50p, and bedtime was 11pm on weekdays and midnight on the weekends.

The Right-wing call for tougher regimes forgets one fact: for these women losing their liberty and their families is the most horrific thing to happen to them.

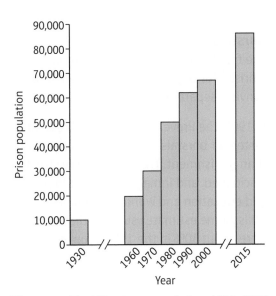

Figure 4.3 The UK prison population, 1930–2015.

Specialised treatment of young offenders

Since 1900, the treatment of young people who break the law has changed significantly.

Timeline

Treatment of young offenders in the 20th century

1900 Borstals introduced

1933 Age of criminal responsibility raised to eight

1948 Criminal Justice Act passed

1963 Age of criminal responsibility raised to ten

1969 Specialised juvenile courts, care orders and supervision orders introduced

1983 Youth custody and youth detention centres replace prison and borstal for under 21s

Borstals

The first borstal was set up in Kent in 1902. This was a prison for boys only. It was designed to keep young convicts separate from older criminals.

In 1908, the Prevention of Crime Act created a national system of borstals. Borstals focused on education rather than punishment. The day was very structured and disciplined, and inmates took part in physical exercise, and education and work programmes teaching practical skills. Some estimates suggest that reoffending rates were about 30% in the 1930s, compared to about 60% in the present day.

In 1982, the Criminal Justice Act abolished the borstal system because it was open to abuse, with force often being used on offenders, rather than counselling. Borstals were replaced with youth custody centres.

Source D

Boys exercising at a borstal in 1937.

Youth justice reforms in the 1940s

The Labour government, which came to power after the Second World War, introduced many radical welfare and social reforms. These included reforms to the youth justice system.

Individuals were also important. Between 1922 and 1947, a prison's commissioner called Alexander Patterson was influential in changing how young offenders were treated. The Criminal Justice Act of 1948 used many of Patterson's ideas. It reduced the use of prison for juveniles, and improved the probation service for young people.

Reforms introduced by the 1948 Criminal Justice Act included:
- convicts were sent to different prisons, depending on the seriousness of the crime and the offender's record
- detention centres were introduced as a deterrent for young offenders – with a more relaxed routine compared to borstals
- attendance centres were used for young people who had committed minor crimes – young offenders attended the centres at weekends for rehabilitation, instead of being detained all week.

Youth justice reforms in the 1960s

The Children and Young Persons Acts of 1963 and 1969 changed the treatment of young offenders in juvenile courts. The 1963 act focused on the importance of caring for and protecting young offenders and raised the age of criminal responsibility from eight to ten years. The 1969 law encouraged offenders to rehabilitate with the support of probation officers and social workers*, over prison sentences.

Key term

Social worker*

State employees who provide help and support to those in society who need it.

Reform and rehabilitation

Changing attitudes in society mean that today, in comparison to the 19th century, many more people think prisoners should be given a chance to change and not simply be punished. Modern courts often use alternative punishments to prison that focus on reform and rehabilitation.

Activities ?

1 Describe a borstal.

2 Look at the alternative punishments below. Choose one example, and explain why it helps to reform a person convicted of a crime.

3 Discuss prison reforms in a small group. Do you think the measures below are better than prison?

Anti-Social Behaviour Order (ASBO)
A court order that places restrictions on what a person can do, e.g. where they can go or who they can talk to. They are usually issued to people who repeatedly behave in an anti-social way, e.g. committing vandalism.

Restorative justice
A criminal meets the victim of their crime, or a relative, to talk about what they have done and understand the impact it has had on others.

Community service
People convicted of minor offences are ordered to do supervised work to improve their local community.

Drug and alcohol treatment programmes
People who have got involved in crime because of a problem with drugs or alcohol are offered help and treatment for their addiction.

Electronic tagging
The court orders a person convicted of a crime to wear an electronic tag. Using the tag, they monitor the criminal's movements. Although the person is not in prison, their movements and activities can be strictly controlled.

Figure 4.4 21st-century alternatives to prison.

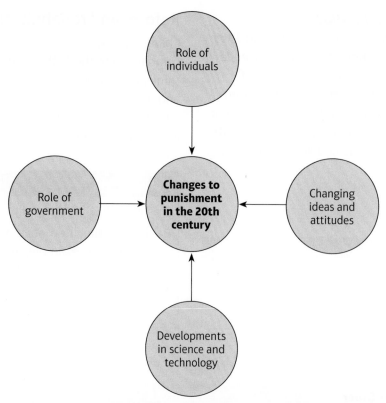

Figure 4.5 Factors influencing changes in punishment since 1900.

Summary

- At the start of the 20th century capital punishment was still used, almost always to punish murder.
- In 1965, capital punishment for murder was abolished.
- The 1940s Labour government introduced many radical welfare and social reforms, such as those affecting young people.
- During the 20th century there were many new ideas about the purpose of prison, and the treatment prisoners should expect in prison.
- Changing attitudes mean that modern courts use alternative punishments to prison for less serious offences.

Checkpoint

Strengthen

S1 Name three factors that contributed to the end of capital punishment for murder in 1965.

S2 Give two examples of alternative punishments to prison in the modern day.

S3 Describe the difference between an open prison and a standard prison.

Challenge

C1 Explain how controversial executions in the 1950s led to the abolition of the death penalty.

C2 In what ways are young offenders treated differently to other offenders in the 21st century?

How confident do you feel about your answers to these questions? Reread the section, then try answering them again.

4.4 Case study: Conscientious objectors in the First and Second World Wars

Conscription in the First World War

In 1914, the First World War broke out and hundreds of thousands of men volunteered to fight. However, by 1916, the numbers of volunteers had gone down, but the army still needed more recruits.

The government introduced **conscription**. This meant that from March 1916, men were forced by law to join the armed forces.

At first the act only applied to unmarried men aged between 18-41, but was later extended to all married men and men up to the age of 51.

Conscription was controversial as, before 1916, service in the armed forces had been voluntary. Now it was illegal to avoid taking part in the war.

Conscientious objectors in the First World War

Some men refused to fight, because they said their conscience would not allow it. They were known as Conscientious Objectors (COs). There were many reasons why men refused to fight.

- Religious reasons, e.g. Quakers were pacifists, which is the name given to people who believe all war is wrong.
- Political reasons – some people disagreed with the aims of the war.
- Some 'absolutists' refused to take any part in the war, as they felt any kind of help in the war effort was wrong.
- Others refused to fight, but were willing to support the war effort in other ways, such as working in factories and farms, or as stretcher bearers – an incredibly dangerous job.

Source A

A 1916 poster explaining the opportunity to seek exemption from conscription into the armed forces.

> # MILITARY SERVICE ACT, 1916
>
> Every man to whom the Act applies will on Thursday, March 2nd, be deemed to have enlisted for the period of the War unless he is excepted or exempt.
>
> ## Any man who has adequate grounds for applying to a Local Tribunal for a
>
> # CERTIFICATE OF EXEMPTION UNDER THIS ACT
>
> ## Must do so BEFORE
>
> # THURSDAY, MARCH 2
>
> Why wait for the Act to apply to you?
>
> Come _now_ and join of your own free will.
>
> You can at once put your claim before a Local Tribunal _for exemption_ from being called up for Military Service if you wish.
>
> # ATTEST NOW
>
> Published by the PARLIAMENTARY AND JOINT LABOUR RECRUITING COMMITTEE, LONDON.   POSTER No. 156.

Tribunals

The Military Service Act did allow people to object to 'joining up'. It included a section called the conscience clause which allowed men to ask for exemption on the grounds of conscience. Some 16,500 men made this request, and had to appear before a special court, called a tribunal, to judge if their claims were genuine.

The tribunals were not always fair because:

- tribunals were held locally, and trials were different depending on who made the decisions
- members of the panels were generally too old to be called up themselves, but often had very clear views about other people's duty to fight.

Treatment of COs

Many absolutists who refused to support the war in any way were imprisoned. Sometimes they faced solitary confinement so they could not mix with other prisoners. The authorities hoped this would make them change their mind.

Some COs were punished by being sent to France, to the front line of the fighting. Once there, they were given orders, and if they refused to follow them they were sentenced by a military court. A small number were sentenced to death. The prime minister intervened to stop this happening, and reduced the punishment to ten years of imprisonment.

Source B

COs in a quarry on Dartmoor. About 1,000 COs were imprisoned at the prison on Dartmoor and made to work in the local granite quarries.

Source C

Jack Foister, a CO in the First World War, describes being sentenced to death at a court martial on 14 June 1916. His sentence was later reduced to ten years of imprisonment.

```
I was brought from the cell to the office
and stood at attention in front of a table
at which three officers were seated. The one
in the centre lectured me quietly but firmly
on the sin of disobeying orders on active
service, said he was going to give me an
order, if I did not obey, I should be court-
martialled for disobedience, the punishment
for which could be sentence of death. There
was a soldier standing to attention in the
same office. The order given me was to fall
in behind this soldier for drill. "Right
turn, quick march," came the order. There
was no response. The greatest strain that
I ever experienced was when that order was
given because I knew it was the final point
and I was the first one to be given the
order and my mind went quickly round. Will
the others do what I am going to do? But it
was all in a flash you see. I didn't have
minutes to think about it... a couple of
seconds. I was not going to fall in. I was
ready to do whatever happened.
```

Why were COs treated so harshly?

The casualty rate of soldiers in the First World War was so high that the government wanted to stop pacifist ideas spreading. They needed to recruit lots of men, and wanted to prevent a wide resistance movement against the war from growing.

- The government presented fighting as a man's duty to his country.
- Refusing to fight was presented as 'unmanly' and even traitorous.
- The press also spread views of COs as cowardly and unpatriotic. The harsh punishments handed out to COs were publicised to put people off refusing to fight.
- Most people had close family and friends who were fighting and who had been killed or injured. They often felt that COs were avoiding their responsibilities.

Some COs and their families were isolated by friends and neighbours. Some received hate mail or white feathers in the post, which were a symbol of cowardice.

Source D

First World War postcard portraying COs as scared to fight and not 'real men'.

Key term

Peace Pledge Union*

An organisation founded in the 1930s that opposed war and sought to find peaceful means to resolve conflicts around the world.

Changes in treatment of COs during the Second World War

During the Second World War (1939–45), COs were offered alternative occupations such as farm work. Prison was generally used as a last resort.

However, those who actively campaigned against the war could find themselves in court. For example, members of an organisation called the Peace Pledge Union*, who posted anti-war posters, were put on trial, but their case was dismissed by the judge.

Changes in social attitudes

During the Second World War, official attitudes to COs were quite different from the First World War. In the Second World War people were being asked to unite against Hitler and Nazism because they persecuted people who opposed them and vulnerable groups. This meant harsh punishments for COs would have been seen as hypocritical.

However, public opinion could still be hostile towards people who refused to fight, when many felt they were making great sacrifices for the war.

Some COs were verbally abused in public – or even attacked. Others lost their jobs, because their employers disapproved of their actions.

Source E

Joyce Allen was a member of the Peace Pledge Union (PPU). Here she describes what happened after she decided to register as a CO.

"When conscription came in I was teaching. I could have asked for exemption, but I wanted to register as a CO... [Even though the school wanted to sack me they] didn't get rid of me: it was difficult to get staff then. I had over 40 supportive letters – the bulk of them from men in the RAF! I think they were scared out of their wits, these young chaps dropping bombs, and wished they could get out of it. The man who was giving me Latin lessons, though, refused to teach me. A member of the PPU offered to teach me instead, and she put the fee I paid her into the PPU funds."

Activities ?

1 Read Source E. Note down two examples of how others reacted to Joyce's decision to be a conscientious objector.

2 In small groups, roleplay a conversation with Joyce. Come up with a list of questions about her views and the reasons why she was a conscientious objector. Practise asking Joyce the questions to see how she would answer.

Exam-style question, Section B

Explain one way in which treatment of witchcraft in the period 1500–1750 was similar to the treatment of conscientious objection in the 20th century. **4 marks**

Exam tip

For this question you should identify a similarity and add information from both periods to support it. You could show knowledge of the actions of either the authorities or the general public.

Summary

- Some men refused to fight in the war as they said their conscience would not allow it. After 1916 they were viewed as criminals.
- The Military Service Act included a section called 'the conscience clause' which allowed men to refuse conscription on the grounds of conscience. Very few were granted this exemption.
- Prison was the most common punishment for COs who refused war work in the First World War.
- In the Second World War, government attitudes to COs were less harsh, but public opinion was generally still hostile.

Checkpoint

Strengthen

S1 Name two punishments faced by COs in the First World War.

S2 Give two examples of work carried out by conscientious objectors during the First World War.

S3 What was the Peace Pledge Union?

Challenge

C1 Explain why the 1916 Conscription Law was so controversial.

C2 Explain why the government treated conscientious objectors so harshly during the First World War.

How confident do you feel about your answers to these questions? Discuss any you are unsure about with a partner then try rewriting your answers together.

4.5 Case study: The Derek Bentley case and the abolition of capital punishment

Learning outcomes

- Understand the main issues in the Derek Bentley criminal trial.
- Evaluate the role the Bentley case played in the debate about ending capital punishment in the UK.

During the 1950s, a number of controversial executions meant the public became increasingly critical of capital punishment. One of these was the case of Derek Bentley, a young man found guilty of murder and executed in 1953.

The Bentley case and public opinion

Many people in Britain disagreed with the sentence. On the night of the execution, 5,000 protestors met outside Wandsworth Prison chanting, 'Murder!' There were angry confrontations with police, and protestors ripped down and burned the death notice posted on the prison gates.

Derek Bentley's family used the media to promote their cause, and through songs, films and books his case became widely known. The Bentley family campaigned for over 40 years. Derek Bentley was eventually pardoned* in 1993, and in 1998 the conviction for murder was quashed*.

Source A

Derek Bentley's parents, sister and brother, on their way to an appeal hearing in London. The appeal was unsuccessful and Bentley was hanged in 1953.

Key terms

Pardon*

To let a person off the punishment after they have been convicted of a crime; or, as in this case, an official acknowledgement that the punishment was unjust.

Quashed*

When a legal sentence is cancelled and no longer recognised, because it is now considered unjust

131

Source B

Photograph of PC Sidney Miles who was killed in 1952. Derek Bentley was executed for his murder.

Key term

Joint enterprise*

When an accomplice to a crime is held jointly responsible for the crime.

Derek Bentley trial, December 1952

Victim – Sidney Miles, policeman, shot during an attempted burglary.

Accused

Christopher Craig
16 years old, fired the gun that killed the policeman.

Derek Bentley
18 years old, there when the murder took place but did not fire the gun, mental age of 10.

What happened?

- Eighteen-year-old Derek Bentley, and his 16-year-old friend Christopher Craig broke into a warehouse on 2 November 1952.
- Craig was armed with a pistol and Bentley was armed with a knuckle-duster which he did not use.
- Bentley had significant learning difficulties.
- Neighbours spotted the pair breaking into the building and called the police.
- Policemen Frederick Fairfax was the first to arrive. He ordered Craig to hand over the gun, to which Bentley replied "Let him have it".
- Craig shot Fairfax and wounded him. Other policemen arrived, including PC Sidney Miles. Craig shot Miles in the head and killed him.
- Both Bentley and Craig were arrested.

Case for the prosecution

- Craig fired the gun. Bentley shouted "Let him have it." This makes him jointly responsible for the murder as he encouraged Craig.
- Bentley has a history of criminality – has been in youth detention.
- Bentley has a low level of intelligence but was not insane and was aware of, and responsible for, his actions.

Case for defence

- "Let him have it" could mean, "Let the policeman have the gun." There are questions about whether he really said it.
- Bentley didn't have a weapon and handed himself over to the police.
- Bentley has a learning disability and a mental age of 10.

Jury

Finds Craig and Bentley guilty, recommends mercy for Bentley.

Judge's sentence

Craig can't be hanged as under 18. Sentenced to long prison term.
Bentley is guilty of the murder under joint enterprise* law. Sentenced to death by hanging.

Figure 4.6 Outline of the Derek Bentley case.

Impact in parliament

David Maxwell Fyfe, the Home Secretary at the time of the Bentley trial, declared: 'There is no possibility of an innocent man being hanged in this country'. However, 200 Members of Parliament (MPs) supported a parliamentary motion calling for Bentley's reprieve*, but before they could debate the motion the death sentence was carried out.

In 1957, changes were made to the law regarding murder. The Homicide Act made allowances for defendants suffering from diminished responsibility*. In these cases, the murder charge would be reduced to manslaughter, which was not punishable by death. In 1965, the death penalty for murder was suspended, and this change was made permanent in 1969.

Key terms

Reprieve*

To cancel or postpone a punishment, especially the death penalty.

Diminished responsibility*

Not being fully in control of your actions, for example, because of a mental illness.

THINKING HISTORICALLY **Change and continuity (4b&c)**

The bird's eye view

Development	Example of short-term changes	Example of change in the long-term
The execution of Derek Bentley.		The death penalty in the UK has not been reintroduced despite significant public support for it to be brought back.

Imagine you are looking at the whole of history using a zoomed-out digital map. You can see the sweep of developments and their consequences, but you cannot see much detail. If you zoom in to the time of the abolition of the death penalty, you can see the event in detail, but will know nothing of its consequences in the long-term in determining opinions about the role of capital punishment in the UK.

Look at the table above and answer the following:

1 What were the short-term changes brought about by Bentley's execution? Write down at least two changes that could complete that column in the table.

2 What changes can you note down in the long-term, e.g. decades after Bentley's execution?

3 Write a paragraph explaining the consequences of Bentley's execution, including both the short-term and the long-term changes.

Summary

- Derek Bentley and Christopher Craig were convicted of the murder of Sidney Miles, a policeman who was shot during an attempted burglary. Only Bentley was executed as Craig was too young.
- The case was controversial and led to an increase in the number of people questioning the death penalty.
- Many MPs at the time believed that Bentley should not be hanged.

Checkpoint

Strengthen

S1 Why was Christopher Craig imprisoned rather than hanged?

S2 Describe the changes to the law on executions after Bentley's death.

S3 Explain why many felt Bentley's execution was wrong.

Challenge

C1 Why do you think it often takes a case like Bentley's to lead to a change in the law? Can you think of other similar examples recently? Discuss with a partner.

Recap: c1900–present: Crime, punishment and law enforcement in recent times

Recall quiz

1. Name two types of driving offences.
2. Define the term 'hate crime'.
3. When did rape in marriage become recognised as a crime in law?
4. What is PCSO an abbreviation of?
5. Who were detained in borstals?
6. What were court hearings for conscientious objectors called?
7. When was Derek Bentley pardoned?
8. What does 'age of criminal responsibility' mean?
9. What is biometric screening used for?
10. Where was the first 'open prison' in the UK?

Activity ?

Illustrated timeline

Create your own illustrated timeline to revise this period. This will help you to visualise the key events, change and continuity with only a few words. You will need a large sheet of paper (A3 or larger). You could illustrate the timeline with images to help you remember what you've learned.

Copy the timeline below. Then, go back through this chapter and add notes to represent the changes in each section, which are: attitudes to crime, definitions of crime, methods of punishment and law enforcement since 1900.

You could do the same for the other chapters of this book to create a revision aid for the whole topic.

	Attitudes to crime	Definitions of crime	Law enforcement	Punishment
1900s	1916–1918 – During the First World War, men who refuse to fight are shunned by society.	1916 – The Military Service Act requires all eligible men to fight. Those who refuse are punished.	1916–1918 – Conscientious objectors attend a tribunal to determine if their grounds for objection are genuine.	1916–1918 – Tribunals send many conscientious objectors to prison.
	1960s – Attitude of society becomes increasingly liberal.	1960s – Attitude of society becomes increasingly liberal.		1960s – Death penalty suspended.
Present ↓				

135

Writing historically: a well-structured response

Every response you write needs to be clearly written and structured. To help you achieve this, you need to give clear signs about how you are answering the question.

Learning outcomes

By the end of this lesson, you will understand how to:

- use your writing to show chronological order
- use your writing to show how you are structuring your answer.

Definition

Chronological: following the order in which events took place.

How can I signal the order of chronological events?

When you explain or describe a process, such as the development of more humane punishments, you can use words to signal the **chronological** order of events.

Look at this sequence of events:

> From c1900 more alternatives to prisons were starting to be discussed.
>
> In 1907 probation officers were employed to check on offenders living outside prison.
>
> By 1922 there was an increased focus on prisoner welfare and education opportunities.
>
> In 1933 there was new focus on preparing prisoners for life after serving their sentence.
>
> The first open prison at New Hall, Wakefield was set up in 1933. Open prisons offered a more relaxed regime. Prisoners were allowed out on day release to work and prepare them to rejoin society.

1. Write a paragraph about the development of more humane punishments using the points above and as many of the words below as possible to signal clearly the order of these events.

> firstly... secondly... then... soon... next... meanwhile... eventually... finally...

How can I signal the structure of my argument?

You can use words like these below to link your ideas and guide the reader through your argument. For example:

> similarly... for example... such as... however... therefore... consequently...
>
> moreover... nonetheless... furthermore... on the other hand... in addition... above all...
>
> significantly... in conclusion...

2. Now look at these two extracts from a response to the following exam-style question. Make a note of all the words from the box above the writer has used to link their ideas and structure their argument.

> 'The impact of science and new technology since 1800 has revolutionised crime detection methods'. How far do you agree? **(16 marks)**

> For most of the 19th century, police could do little to detect criminals and relied on catching criminals in the act. Consequently, traditional approaches such as relying on eye witness testimony remained common. However, scientific breakthroughs like the discovery of DNA meant that crime scenes could hold evidence to place a person at the crime location...
>
> Science and technology were, therefore, a key factor in improvements in crime detection. There are, on the other hand, other factors to consider...

Did you notice?

These signal words can be positioned at a number of different points in a sentence.

3. At what point in the sentences above are most of the signal words positioned – at the start of the sentence, the middle of the sentence, or the end of the sentence?

Improving an answer

Now look at the final paragraph below, which is a response to the same exam-style question as earlier:

> Both of these factors are interdependent and important. The scientific and technological breakthroughs of the 19th and 20th centuries (fingerprinting, computer data systems and DNA) were the more fundamental. The funding of the new police computer systems by government also had a huge impact on crime detection methods. Without it these breakthroughs would have had considerably less impact.

4. Rewrite this conclusion, using some of the words from the box at the top of this page to signal the structure of the argument clearly.

Preparing for your GCSE Paper 1 exam

Paper 1 overview

Your Paper 1 is in two sections, which examine the Historic Environment and the Thematic Study. Together they count for 30% of your History assessment. The questions on the Thematic Study: Crime and punishment in Britain, c1000–present, are in Section B and are worth 20% of your History assessment. Allow two-thirds of the examination time for Section B. There are an extra four marks for Spelling, Punctuation and Grammar (SpaG) in the last question.

History Paper 1	Historic Environment and Thematic Depth Study			Time 1 hour 15 mins
Section A	Historic Environment	Answer 3 questions	16 marks	25 mins
Section B	Thematic Study	Answer 3 questions	32 marks + 4 SpaG marks	50 mins

Section B: Crime and punishment in Britain, c1000–present

You will answer Questions 3 and 4, and then **either** Question 5 or Question 6.

Q3 Explain one way... (4 marks)

You are given about half a page of lines to write about a **similarity** or a **difference**. Allow five minutes to write your answer.

This question is worth just four marks so keep the answer brief. Only one comparison is needed. You should **compare** by referring to both periods named in the question – for example, 'xxx was similar because in the Middle Ages… and also in the 16th century…'

Q4 Explain why... (12 marks)

This question asks you to explain the reasons **why something happened**. Allow about 15 minutes to write your answer.

You are given two information points as prompts to help you. You do not have to use the prompts and you will not lose marks by leaving them out. Higher marks are gained by adding in a point not covered in the prompts.

You will be given at least two pages of lines for your answer in the booklet. This does not mean you should try to fill all the space. Aim to write an answer giving at least three well-explained reasons.

Q5 OR Q6 How far do you agree...? (16 marks + 4 marks for SpaG)

This question, including SPaG, is worth 20 marks – more than half the marks for the whole of the Thematic Study. Be sure to keep 30 minutes of the exam time to answer it and to check your spelling, punctuation and grammar.

You can **choose** between Questions 5 and 6. You will have prompts to help as for Question 4.

The statement can be about the concepts of: significance, cause, consequence, change, continuity, similarity, difference. Try and think about which concept to use to answer the question.

You should think about **both** sides of the argument. Plan your answer before you begin to write, putting your points under two headings: 'For' and 'Against'. Make a point and then support it with details from your own knowledge.

In this question, four extra marks are given for good spelling, punctuation and grammar. Use full sentences, paragraphs, capital letters, commas and full stops, etc. Try also to use the specialist terms you have learned, e.g. 'retribution'.

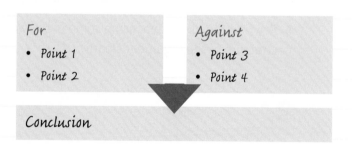

For
- Point 1
- Point 2

Against
- Point 3
- Point 4

Conclusion

Paper 1, Questions 3 & 4

Explain **one** way in which conditions in prisons were different in the mid 19th and late 20th centuries. **(4 marks)**

Basic answer

Conditions in prisons in the 19th century were very harsh. They used the separate system to punish prisoners. Then in the late 20th century prisoners were allowed to mix and some prisons were open-style prisons.

This answer identifies different treatment in prisons in each period but the examples are vague. The word 'then' shows some recognition of difference but the detail of the difference is not spelled out.

5th

Verdict

This is a basic answer because:

- the candidate has provided very general comments about the differences in prisons between the two periods
- the candidate has not been clear about the difference – the answer says 19th century conditions were harsh but does not say they were less harsh in the 20th century.

Use the feedback to rewrite this answer, making as many improvements as you can.

Why were there changes in criminal activity in the years c1900 to the present day?

You may use the following information in your answer:

- *transport*
- *the internet.*

You **must** also use information of your own. **(12 marks)**

Basic answer

From 1900 to the present day there were many changes in crime. Some people use computers to steal money. Other people use new transport for doing crimes. For example, they steal expensive cars to sell on or drive really fast and break speed limits. In the past they went by horse or walked and there weren't speed limits. Nowadays more people think it's wrong to speed because of accidents.

There should be more focus on the factors leading to change and less description. Factors of society's attitudes and new technology have been mentioned, but should be explained in more detail.

6th

Since the internet was invented some people use it for stealing money from internet bank accounts or getting in touch with other criminals.

There is an attempt to structure the answer, but it should be better organised – material on the internet is mentioned in two separate paragraphs.

Verdict

This is a basic answer because:

- it describes the changes, rather than explaining why they happened
- the answer mentions talk about changes in technology as a factor, but ideally needed to mention another two
- the answer needs more structure. Each different factor should be in a separate paragraph.

Use the feedback to rewrite this answer, making as many improvements as you can.

Paper 1, Questions 3 & 4

Explain **one** way in which conditions in prisons were different in the mid 19th and late 20th centuries. **(4 marks)**

Good answer

In the mid 19th century conditions were harsh. Prisons like Pentonville used the 'separate' system. Prisoners lived in individual cells and were not allowed to talk to or even see each other. They were made to do hard work as a punishment and as a deterrent to other criminals.

In the late 20th century prisoners were allowed to talk to each other. They did work but this was to help them learn a trade so they could earn a living when they left, not a punishment. Conditions were much less harsh.

This answer describes treatment in prisons in both centuries. It gives specific examples of treatment and points out the differences between the two periods.

Verdict

This is a good answer because it uses specific information about the topic to demonstrate differences in the prison system in both periods.

Why were there changes in criminal activity in the years, c1900 to the present day? **(12 marks)**

Good answer

A range of factors led to criminal activity changing over the last two hundred years: social attitudes, new technology and new types of transport have all been important.

This answer begins with a clear focus on the question.

New technologies have had a great impact on changing criminal activities. For example, new cars are much faster than previous transport. This has led the authorities to introduce speeding laws to make roads safer. Speeding became a crime in the 20th century. So another reason why criminal activity changed is that new laws created new crimes.

The reasons for change are clearly shown. The answer combines new technology with the role of government action.

Social attitudes have also played a significant part. Previously violence and control of your wife was seen as acceptable. By the 1970s with the rise of the women's rights movement domestic violence was criminalised.

A new factor, not mentioned in the bullet points, is clearly explained.

So overall, transport, the internet and changing social attitudes have all played an important part in change in criminal activity. Social attitudes have led to changes in what is criminalised. The internet has completely changed the methods by which criminals can operate on a large often international scale.

The candidate has addressed the question directly in the conclusion, distinguishing between different factors affecting change.

Verdict

This is a good answer because:
- it has included only relevant information and used it to support valid points
- the explanation is analytical, related to the factors
- the line of reasoning is consistently developed throughout the answer.

Paper 1, Question 5/6

'Attitudes in society were the most important factor influencing how criminal activity was dealt with in the period c1500–c2000'.

How far do you agree? Explain your answer. You may use the following information in your answer:

- laws against witchcraft in the 16th century
- conscientious objectors in the 20th century.

You **must** also use information of your own. **(16 marks + 4 for SPaG)**

Exam tip

Consider points for and against the statement and make a judgement. Be clear about your reasons for agreeing or disagreeing. SPaG is also assessed. Take care with spelling, punctuation and the use of sentences, paragraphs and historical terms.

Basic answer

Attitudes in society changed from 1500–2000. A good example of this is witchcraft. In the past, witches could be executed, but now no-one believes in witches anymore so it's not seen as a crime.

> The answer is broadly correct, but it's too vague and needs some specific examples of how and why attitudes changed.

In World War I COs were affected by changes in social attitudes. In society COs were treated as cowards and the public often supported harsh punishments for those who refused to fight. Public opinion was very harsh and COs who refused war work were sometimes disowned by their own friends and families.

> There is some analysis of the importance of social attitudes, but the treatment is descriptive and not analytical.

> Change in the way the law dealt with conscientious objectors in the Second World War is not included.

Other factors were also important. For the treatment of witches, the power of the king was important. James I was keen to hunt witches and wanted them punished harshly. He wrote a book that explained how to run a witch trial. Therefore, social attitudes were important but there were other factors too.

> A stronger paragraph with good focus on the question. But the role of the king needs further development and the answer does not make an overall judgement, except for the last brief comment.

Verdict

This is a basic answer because:

- it includes some valid information but does not provide enough specific examples or analyse factors enough to be a strong answer
- the answer does not go beyond the prompts given and it deals only with the beginning and end of the period
- there is some analysis of the question but this is not consistent throughout and the answer lacks a clear overall judgement based on clear criteria.

Use the feedback to rewrite this answer, making as many improvements as you can.

Paper 1, Question 5/6

'Attitudes in society were the most important factor influencing how criminal activity was dealt with in the period c1500–c2000'.

How far do you agree? Explain your answer. **(16 marks + 4 for SPaG)**

Good answer

Attitudes in society did have a big impact on how criminal activity was dealt with from 1500–2000.

Social attitudes are significant in explaining how the crime of witchcraft was dealt with. Society used to treat witches quite positively, viewing them as wise women who could give help and advice on childbirth or illness. However, the attitudes of society changed as Henry VIII and James I treated witchcraft as much more of a problem. Ordinary attitudes changed to reflect these changes in the law. Many ordinary people co-operated with Matthew Hopkins's witch hunts in the mid 17th century. Many people were tried for witchcraft and over a hundred were executed. This example shows that social attitudes could have a significant impact on how crimes were dealt with.

Government and social attitudes disagreed over smuggling. Although the government tried to make smuggling a crime for much of this time period, many people ignored the law and continued to smuggle, or to buy goods from smugglers. This is because smuggling was a 'social crime' and they didn't think there was anything wrong with it. This shows how it's difficult for the government to enforce the law if the attitude of society disagrees. It was easier for the government to enforce laws against conscientious objectors during the First and Second World Wars, however, because the public believed it was the duty of people to fight and protect their country.

So to conclude, social attitudes had an important impact on how crimes were dealt with during this 500-year period. Although sometimes the role of government has been more important in influencing society's views, really the law can only work if social attitudes agree with it as shown by attitudes towards smuggling.

The answer begins with a clear focus on the question.

Good knowledge used to explain the link between change in attitudes and how witchcraft was dealt with.

Individual paragraphs and the overall answer follow a clear structure. The conclusion gives clear criteria for judgement.

The evidence selected to support the analysis shows a strong grasp of the wider context.

The example goes beyond the bullet point prompts and the paragraph makes a clear, relevant point.

Verdict

This is a good answer because:
- the answer keeps a clear focus on the role of attitudes in society, backed by a range of good knowledge
- criteria for reaching the judgement have been set out and applied throughout
- there is a clear line of reasoning running through a well-organised answer.

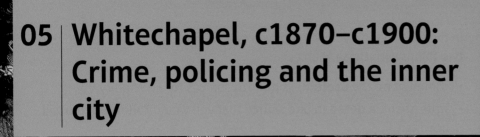

05 | Whitechapel, c1870–c1900: Crime, policing and the inner city

In the late 19th century, Britain was one of the richest countries in the world, but Whitechapel in the East End of London was extremely poor. There were many beggars, prostitutes, criminals and alcoholics. Even many of those who did work were close to being plunged back into poverty.

For many women prostitution was often their only choice other than a life in the workhouse.

Whitechapel, with its crowded slums and dark alleyways, was an extremely difficult environment for the police to operate in. The founder of the Salvation Army described the slums as 'a dark continent full of nameless loathing where lawlessness still reigns supreme'.

In 1888, a series of gruesome killings in Whitechapel by 'Jack the Ripper' led to a media frenzy, and the police came under intense scrutiny.

This section will look in more detail at Whitechapel and the actions of H Division of the Metropolitan Police.

Learning outcomes

By the end of this chapter, you will:

- know about the context of national and regional policing in the late 19th century
- understand the local context and problems of Whitechapel in the late 19th century
- know about problems caused by immigration and a fluctuating population
- know about the organisation of policing in Whitechapel in the late 19th century
- know about methods of investigative policing available in the late 19th century
- understand how to use sources and ask appropriate questions in your enquiry into crime, policing and the inner city.

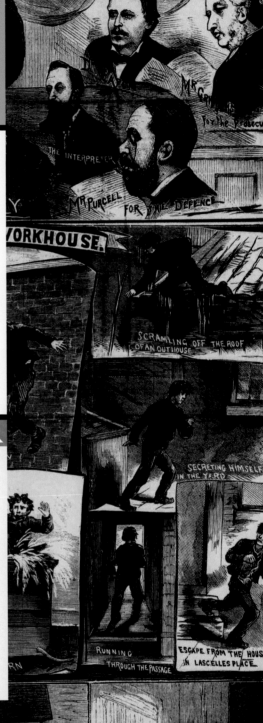

Sources, information and evidence

In the examination you will be given **two** sources, and you are asked to do **two** things with these sources:

- comment on the **usefulness of both** sources for an enquiry
- write about: **a detail in one source** that you would **follow up**. You will need to:
  - consider the question you would ask about that detail
  - consider what type of source might provide an answer to that
  - explain why that type of source helps to answer the question.

Because most of the marks in this section of the examination are for your work with sources, there are more sources in this chapter than in the rest of the book. Sources A and B in this section are examples to help you understand how the examination works.

Source A is about living conditions in the Spitalfields area of Whitechapel. It comes from a book by Howard Goldsmid, published in 1886, called *Dottings of a Dosser*. Goldsmid wanted to describe living conditions worse than any that had previously been reported in newspapers. The source describes the scene in Flower and Dean Street, Spitalfields.

Source B is about an event in 1887 known as 'Bloody Sunday' when the Metropolitan Police ('the Met') attempted to stop a demonstration in Trafalgar Square. The protestors were dissatisfied with government policy on a number of issues including unemployment. Public meetings like this had been banned by the Home Secretary just a few days before. Trafalgar Square is in central London, but many of the demonstrators and police officers, including members of H Division (the Whitechapel branch of the Met), came from Whitechapel.

Key term

Socialist League*

A political group, set up in 1885, that campaigned for workers' rights.

Source B

This pamphlet was printed by the Socialist League*, after Alfred Linnell was run down by police horseman and killed while protesting in Trafalgar square in 1887.

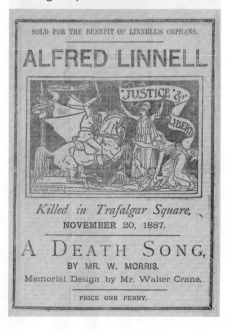

Source A

From *Dottings of a Dosser* by Howard Goldsmid, published in 1886.

There is a level of society even lower than that of the poor people who herd together in noisy courts and filthy alleys full of human excrement [waste]. They are the unfortunates, whose only home is the doss house, who have for many years not known what it is to have the shelter of a room, except in a common lodging house. There is not yet a bitter cry from these as up to now they have found no spokesman to echo it in the ear of the public. In one house, called 'Little Wonder', all are as ill-looking as one could meet in a lifetime. The women are in many ways worse than the men. Their language is more obscene, their habits more filthy and they seem to enjoy this situation.

Usefulness (utility)

No source is useful (or useless) until you have an enquiry. Our enquiry is:

How useful are Sources A and B for an enquiry into the problems police faced in dealing with desperately poor people in East London in the 1880s?

To answer this question, you will need to explain the criteria* for your judgement, based on your analysis of the content, provenance and context of the source. You should also consider asking how useful each of these makes the source.

Key terms

Criteria* (singular: criterion)
Benchmarks by which you judge something. It is vital that you know your criteria before judging a historical source.

Context*
The wider setting. Historical context means the other information available on the same topic.

Provenance*
Where a source comes from – who made it, when and why.

Criteria	Questions you might ask about the source
Content	What does the source tell you?
Provenance	What was the original purpose of the source?
Context*	How does the source fit in with what you already know about East London in the 1880s?

How does this work in practice?

Content
Source A tells us that housing conditions were terrible and that the streets were just as bad, with alleyways filled with human waste. It suggests that unrest might follow if the conditions are not improved.

Provenance*
Source A is written by a person searching for powerful evidence to make an impact on readers of his book. Since we are told that Goldsmid was trying to find worse conditions than journalists had previously reported, he is probably selecting his evidence carefully. This selection may be part of an attempt to exaggerate conditions, which might lead us to question how truthful it is.

Context
Always try to use your knowledge to evaluate the source. This is known as 'context'. When you have studied this topic a bit more, you could show how this source fits into your knowledge by pointing out that there were particularly bad areas in Spitalfields, but also some parts that had been rebuilt and improved. Or you could link Goldsmid's fears of what might happen if the people found leaders to speak for them, to the rise of a group of politicians who came to have influence over the first London County Council.

Activities ?

1 Make a list of questions you could ask of Source B to judge its usefulness.

2 Using the categories from Figure 5.1, make a list of sources that could be used to study your life.

    a Give at least one example source in each category.

    b Explain why each example would be useful.

Following up on a source

Where possible, historians try to use as many different types of source as they can. There is a good reason for this. Each different type of source has different strengths and weaknesses.

The second question about sources asks you to pick a detail from one of the sources and then explain how you would follow up that detail with a different type of source. Figure 5.1 shows the range of different types of source a historian can use.

Source C

A dramatic picture of the events of 'Bloody Sunday', 13 November 1887. It appeared in the *Illustrated London News*, a weekly newspaper, a few days after the events shown.

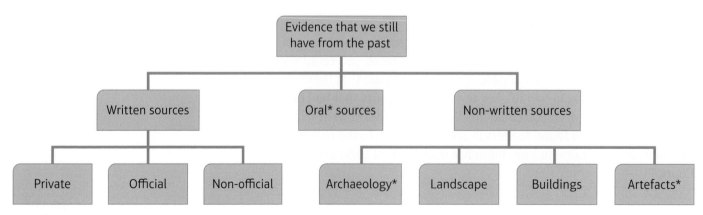

Figure 5.1 Types of source used by historians.

Provenance

Historians think very carefully about their sources. They test them to check whether they are really appropriate for the way they want to use them. The tests are:

What is its purpose?

When, where and why was the source created, and who by? When we read something about living in the 19th century by someone who was there, it helps to know if they wrote this at the time or 50 years later. But just because it was written at the time doesn't mean it is true. A policeman on the beat in Whitechapel might have written to his family a couple of days after being set upon with stones by a mob. The purpose of the source might be to reassure his loved ones, rather than to tell the whole truth – that he had been badly hurt.

What is the opinion of the author or artist?

Does the person have a particular point of view? For example, if you are reading a criticism of the Metropolitan Police, it might be useful to know whether it was written by an opponent or a supporter of the government, which was in charge of that police force. Sometimes the police were looked upon as agents of an unpopular government – a kind of government in uniform.

Is the source trying to change people's views?

Propaganda* is deliberately created to change people's views. It might be exaggerated, it might leave things out, or it might just not be true. This doesn't mean historians don't use propaganda – it provides a lot of useful evidence – but the use might be revealing what the government wanted people to believe, rather than what really happened.

Is it part of the action or reflecting on the action?

What is the difference between a live radio commentary on a football match, and an account of that same game written years later in a player's autobiography? Both have their strengths – but they are very different.

Turning a source into evidence

A source is only useful, and it can only be turned into evidence, when you have a question or enquiry. For example, Source B is neither useful nor not useful alone. If we have an enquiry into, for example, either: a) attitudes towards the police in the 1880s, or b) charitable work in London; then we can think about whether it is useful or not. In the case of enquiry a) it is useful, and in the case of enquiry b) it is not.

Key terms

Oral*
Spoken.

Archaeology*
The study of objects found under the ground.

Artefact*
A historical object.

Propaganda*
Deliberate mass persuasion.

Source D

An eye witness account of 'Bloody Sunday' by the artist Walter Crane. He was well known for his support for working people and was a member of the Socialist League.

I never saw anything more like real warfare in my life – only the attack was all on one side. The police, in spite of their numbers, apparently thought they could not cope with the crowd. They had certainly exasperated [extremely annoyed] them, and could not disperse them, as after every charge – and some of these drove the people right against the shutters in the shops in the Strand – they returned again.

Source E

Henry Hamilton Fyfe recalls the events of 'Bloody Sunday' in his autobiography, written in 1935. Hamilton Fyfe was a member of the Conservative Party in 1887, but later changed his political views and stood as a Labour candidate in the 1929 General Election.

When the unemployed dockers marched on Trafalgar Square, where meetings were then forbidden, I enrolled myself as a special constable to defend respectable people against the masses. Wearing an armlet and wielding a baton, I paraded and patrolled and felt proud of myself. My old gentleman at the office [Fyfe's boss at *The Times* newspaper] was a Conservative who seemed to approve of violence. He would have had the unemployed shot down.

Judging sources

Start with the **provenance** (the nature, origin and purpose of the source). Does this suggest strengths or weaknesses when using this source? For example, we don't know if Source C was drawn as propaganda to make a judgement about the police.

Move on to **content**. What can you learn from the source that is relevant? What can you work out from it?

It is easier to use artists' sketches as sources if we know **why** they were drawn. The same is true of photographs taken. Often, we don't know why – so the best you can do is think carefully about the context and content of the drawing or photograph.

THINKING HISTORICALLY   Evidence (1b&c)

The message and the messenger

There are many sources of information about the past. Historians use these sources to help them draw conclusions.

Study Sources B, C, D and E (pages 144 to 148) about a demonstration in Trafalgar Square in 1887. Now read Source F in Section 5.1 (page 154). In this source, Sir Charles Warren, the head of the Metropolitan Police, says a number of things. He was writing for a popular magazine that he knew would be:

a   read by important politicians

b   discussed by many people around the country

c   available to his bosses at the Home Office (the government department in charge of the Met).

What information does the source contain? What was Sir Charles saying? Answer the following questions to find out.

1   Which group does he say have allowed many riots to occur?

2   What does he say has been the effect on peaceful citizens?

3   Who does he say has supported the rioters?

Historians are not usually interested in information for its own sake. Historians are interested in using information to work out answers to questions about the past. Use the information you have just taken from the source, and the information about its context provided above the source, to try to work out answers to the following questions.

4   What do you think that Sir Charles wanted his bosses to think when they read his letter?

5   What can we tell about Sir Charles's views about politicians from the fact that he wrote these words for a public audience in 1888?

As a historian investigating the performance of the Metropolitan Police during the troubles of 1887–88:

6   what evidence might you look for in responses to Sir Charles's letter by the magazine's readers?

7   what other types of sources might you want to look at to gather evidence?

Activities ?

In groups, consider the enquiry: 'Was the treatment by police of the protesters in Trafalgar Square a reasonable response?' Study Source E.

1 Think about the provenance of Source E. What do you learn about Fyfe? How might this change how you view the source?

2 What do you learn from the source about police methods?

3 Was the writer of Source E there at the time? Why might this matter?

4 Would Source E have any reason to criticise the methods used against the protesters?

5 Using your answers to these questions, is Source E useful for the enquiry above? Give reasons.

THINKING HISTORICALLY Evidence (2a)

Information and evidence

Information only becomes evidence when we use it to **work something out** about an issue in the past. Information needs to be questioned before we can use it as **evidence** to draw conclusions. Without a question, information doesn't tell us very much.

Study the following questions about 'Bloody Sunday' in Trafalgar Square:

1 How did Alfred Linnell die?	2 What sort of injuries did people in Trafalgar Square receive?	3 Why did the crowd come to Trafalgar Square that day?
4 Who led the protest?	5 How many police were injured?	6 What did people think about the actions of the Metropolitan Police?

Study Sources B to E (pages 144–148).

1 Which of the six questions would the sources **not** help us answer?

2 Which question is Source C most useful in providing evidence for?

Look at Source D. Draw up a table with three columns labelled 'Question', 'Inference' and 'Evidence'.

3 Write out 'How did Alfred Linnell die?' in the first column. Then use Source D to fill in the other two columns with ideas that answer the question, and evidence for this question from Source D.

4 Write out the sixth question in a new row, and add ideas and evidence from Source D.

Look at the ideas you've added from Source D. Are they the same for the two questions?

5 In your own words, explain how the question you ask affects what evidence you use in a source.

How police forces were organised

There were many different police forces at this time. Many counties had their own force, and within counties many cities and towns had separate forces. The Home Secretary, based in Westminster, had little control over local police forces outside London, which were usually run by watch committees*.

Key term

Watch committee*

A group of local politicians or law professionals set up to monitor the work of police forces.

The exception was the Metropolitan Police force in London, which reported directly to the Home Secretary, who also appointed the head of the force. The government didn't want to give up this power. When the London County Council was set up, in 1889, there were discussions about giving it control over the Met; but the government said no.

Manpower

Police work was made harder by not having enough policemen. By 1885, the Met was made up of 13,319 men among a population of just over five million; but only 1,383 of those officers were available for duty at any one time.

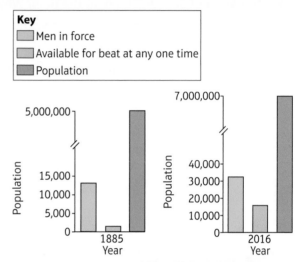

Figure 5.2 Metropolitan Police manpower 1885 and 2016.

Using sources for an enquiry into policing

What sources could help you find out more about policing in Britain in the later 19th century?

Official statistics

Since 2009, the records of more than 1.4 million criminal trials held in England and Wales in the 19th century have been posted online. The National Archive also has statistics for crime and policing.

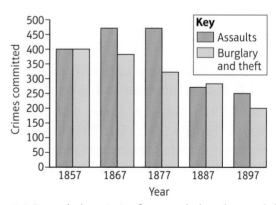

Figure 5.3 Recorded statistics for assault, burglary and theft in England, 1857–1900.

According to the Home Office archive, the detective force in London grew from 216 in 1878 to 294 in 1883, and the number of arrests they made rose from 13,000 to 18,000. For more figures from the archive, see Source A.

Source A

Home Office figures produced in 1881, comparing crime in 1880 with the annual average for 1875–79.

> In examining the crimes in detail and selecting certain of the Indictable Offences for the purpose of a closer comparison, — the Annual Average of the 5 years ended December, 1879, and the Numbers for 1880 are taken. These with but two exceptions show a marked decrease.
>
> The proportions, with the respective figures, are given in the following Table against each selected Offence:—

Crimes.	Annual average for the 5 years 1875 to 1879.	Numbers for 1880.	Increase, or Decrease per Cent.
1. Murder	68	61	− 10·2 per Cent.
2. Shooting at, Stabbing, wounding with intent to maim &c.,	154	123	− 20·1
3. Burglary	330	*425	+ 28·7
4. Robbery, Robbery with Violence, and Assaults to Rob	270	236	− 12·5
5. Larceny from the person	1,256	1,116	− 11·1
6. Larceny, simple	6,123	5,011	− 18·1
7. Receiving stolen goods	452	414	− 8·4
8. Assaults and inflicting bodily harm	902	740	− 17·9
9. Other Offences	6,333	6,644	+ 4·9
Total	15,888	14,770	− 7·0

Police and court records

Statistics from individual police stations are useful, but can be misleading. According to records, during the 1860s, a Middlesbrough policeman could be expected to be assaulted twice a year. But these statistics only cover cases where the officer made an arrest or a report. Can you think of any reasons why a police constable might not have done so?

There are also extensive archives of records from court cases. Many people arrested in Whitechapel found themselves tried at the Central Criminal Court in London – known as the Old Bailey. Source B shows extracts from one such case.

Source B

From the court records of the Central Criminal Court, 12 May 1862.

CONRAD JAGER: I was at a public-house in Fieldgate-street, on Saturday, 22nd February – I left the house about 12 o'clock at night – as I was coming out these three men and Peter Conse fell on me – Eskucken laid hold of me, and Bartels struck me with a key, on the head – I then became insensible [unconscious].

PATRICK GARAGHTY (Policeman, H159): On this night, I saw the row outside the public-house – it was partly quashed [stopped] when I got up – there was another constable there – I saw Bartels go into his own house – I also saw Jager there – we separated them, and then got to the other end of the street, where there was another row, and there we found it necessary to apprehend [arrest] five.

Exam-style question, Section A

How could you follow up Source A to find out more about the problems of policing the Whitechapel neighbourhood in the period 1870–1900?

In your answer, you must give the question you would ask and the type of source you could use.

Complete the table below.   **4 marks**

Detail in Source A that I would follow up:	
Question I would ask:	
What type of source I could use:	
How this might help answer my question:	

Exam tip

Tackle the question in four steps:

- First, pick a detail e.g. there were 61 murders in 1880.
- Next, choose a question, e.g. how many of these murders were solved?
- Then suggest a type of source to use, e.g. arrest records from police stations in those areas.
- Finally, say how this would help answer the question, e.g. the arrest records would reveal if anyone was arrested for any of the murders.

Memoirs and reports

Another useful source of information is police memoirs*. James Bent and Richard Jervis were two Lancashire policemen who wrote accounts of their long careers. Memoirs need to be treated with care, as people tend to use them to present their lives in a positive way, but the Bent and Jervis memoirs do provide a detailed picture of police work in north-west England in the late 19th century. They show that violence between police and locals was common and that poachers (on PC Bent's rural beat) were often part of organised gangs.

Key term

Memoir*

An individual's account of his or her life. It may be based on diaries and other records, or on memory.

Recording crime

The way crimes were recorded is also important, as Source C shows.

Source C

From a report by a government committee on criminal statistics in 1895. The committee is reporting on problems in the police tables of crimes and convictions, which were published each year.

```
The figures have been prepared by the
police with great care, but some forces
have proceeded on one basis and others on
another. The making of an attendance order
[issued when a parent failed to send a child
to school] was treated as a conviction by
121 police forces and excluded from the
returns by 27. This alone added about 20,000
convictions a year to the tables, where
there was in fact no conviction.
```

Crime rates seem to have gone down at the end of the 19th century. Perhaps criminals thought improvements to policing made it more likely that they would be caught. However, this is only speculation and historians are careful about any conclusions they make based on statistics, as you can see in Interpretation 1.

Interpretation 1

From *Crime and Criminals of Victorian London*, by Adrian Gray, published in 2006.

There has been much debate among historians as to whether crime worsened during the Victorian period. Statistics are problematic. There were variations in statistical collection and an improving police force could lead to more arrests. Some activities became illegal that were not before as the State became more regulatory [made more laws]. However despite the occasional scare, there is general consensus that the crime trend in Victorian England was downwards.

Source D is from a Home Office memo that explains how difficult it is to interpret crime statistics.

Source D

A Home Office memo from the 1880s.

Population. The figures in the statistics are absolute figures of crime, without regard to population [i.e. the figures do not assess numbers of crimes against the size of the population]. In the period of 34 years now under review the population has increased about 50%. There has also been an unknown immigration from the countryside...

The media

One of the easiest ways of following what happened is through local and national newspaper accounts. But these publications often valued 'getting a good story' ahead of the facts. The name of the *Illustrated Police News* suggests it was an official publication but in fact it was a 'penny dreadful'* and very anti-police. Its most important purpose was to sell newspapers – rarely letting the truth get in the way of a 'good story'. So negative did some of the press become that, from the 1860s, police newspapers such as the *Police Review*, began to appear. These challenged the negative views of local policemen in other papers.

Source E

An illustration published in a newspaper on 22 September 1888.

...Y FOR THE WHITECHAPEL FIEND. WOMEN SECRETLY ARMED.

Key term

Penny dreadful*

A cheap publication that delighted in shocking readers with gory details of crimes to 'entertain'.

During the Jack the Ripper murders, in October 1888, James Keating, Superintendent of Bethnal Green (a district next to Whitechapel) was asked about his own division's experiences for an article in the *Evening Argus*. Keating described just one serious incident, but left out others, including four stabbings, four robberies with violence, and two serious attacks on women. This example shows why police station statistics need to be consulted as well as newspapers.

Activities ?

1 What does Source B reveal about the kind of incidents policemen had to deal with in Whitechapel?

2 What problems associated with crime statistics are described in Sources C and D?

3 Look at Source E. What could suggest that this is from a 'penny dreadful'? Give reasons for your answer.

The Criminal Investigation Department

Although the main task of the police was to prevent crime, a detective department was added to the Metropolitan Police in 1842. It was tiny and ineffective and there was confusion over whether detectives were meant to prevent or detect crime.

However, in 1878, the Criminal Investigation Department (CID) was created, with 216 officers. This finally seemed to clear up confusions between crime prevention and crime detection. However, detection standards did not improve, as the Ripper investigation showed (see pages 173–182).

Commissioner Charles Warren

Following a series of strikes and demonstrations, the Home Secretary appointed a former general, Sir Charles Warren, as Metropolitan Police Commissioner in 1886. This was probably meant as a warning to those who were seen as troublemaking opponents of the government. But it also made people think the police were just the government in uniform.

It was Commissioner Warren who called in the army to control the protestors in Trafalgar Square on 'Bloody Sunday' (see pages 144–149). The police action on that day added to a growing feeling that the police only cared about the middle and upper classes and not the poor. This made policing in poorer districts much more difficult.

Warren became increasingly unpopular. When Jack the Ripper terrorised Whitechapel a year later, Warren was forced to resign as Commissioner. He made himself even less popular by sharing his views about public disorder in a popular magazine (Source F).

Source F

From a letter by Sir Charles Warren, published November 1888, in *Murray's Magazine*.

Successive governments have not made a stand against the more noisy section of the people representing a small minority, and have allowed many riots to occur that have brought terrorism to peaceful and law-abiding citizens. Leading Opposition politicians, opposed to the present Government, have used these riots to their own advantage by shamefully supporting the mob.

Summary

- Unlike other forces, the Metropolitan Police was controlled directly by the government.
- Following a series of scandals and accusations of incompetence, the CID was set up in 1878.
- Useful sources for investigating policing include: reports from individual police stations, records of court cases, memoirs, and national and local newspapers.
- There are drawbacks as well as advantages to each of these sources – particularly police station reports and newspapers.

Checkpoint

Strengthen

S1 Which government minister was given responsibility for the Metropolitan Police?

S2 Give two examples of problems you might encounter when using records of Victorian criminal offences from local police stations or from memoirs by police officers.

S3 Why can it be difficult for historians to use 'penny dreadfuls' as evidence about the effectiveness of the police in the late 19th century? Try to give at least two reasons.

Challenge

C1 Explain why it is hard for historians to tell whether crime got worse during the late 19th century.

How confident do you feel about your answers to these questions? If you are unsure, form a group with other students, discuss the answers then record your conclusions. Your teacher can give you some hints.

5.2 The local context of Whitechapel

Learning outcomes

- Know about the nature and impact of poor housing conditions.
- Know about attempts to improve housing and provision for the poor in workhouses.
- Understand the links between unemployment, inner-city poverty, immigration and crime.

In the late 19th century, Whitechapel, in the East End of London, was one of the capital's poorest districts. Out of a population of 30,000, perhaps 1,000 were homeless. Long-established Londoners shared the district with more recent Irish and Jewish Eastern European immigrants. There were high levels of crime.

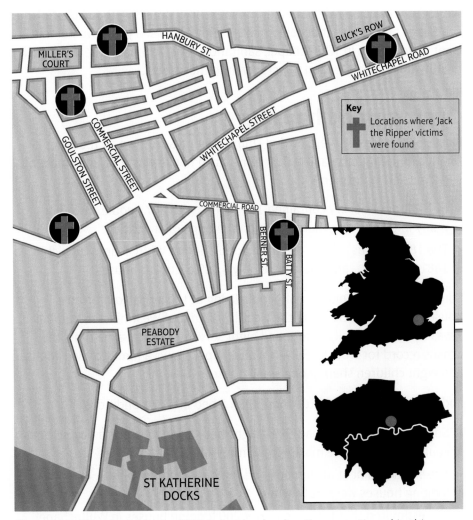

Figure 5.4 Whitechapel in the 1880s, showing key locations mentioned in this chapter.

Features of Whitechapel	Problems and crimes	See pages
Overcrowded accommodation	Theft of personal property, domestic abuse	156–157
Unreliable work, unemployment	Stealing, disruptive behaviour	158
Prostitution	Assaults on women, gangs intimidating women	169
Alcoholism	Disorder on the streets, especially around public houses	151 (Source B), 169
Workhouses	Theft and other crimes committed by people desperate not to go to the workhouse	158–159
Orphans	Petty crimes, begging	160
Immigration	Tension and violence between longer-established residents and Irish and Jewish immigrants	161–163

Pollution and poor sanitation

Whitechapel was heavily polluted. The maze-like streets were full of stinking gas fumes and smoke that could make it difficult to see your own hand in front of your face. In Whitechapel, sanitation* was very poor. There was little healthy drinking water and sewers ran into the streets.

Overcrowded housing

Most housing was in overcrowded slum areas – also known as 'rookeries' – famous for being dirty and full of crime. Each house was split into smaller, very crowded, apartments.

- In 1877, one rookery contained 123 rooms, with 757 people, including many families living there, some on the brink of starvation.
- The 1881 census* shows the total population of Whitechapel District in 1881 as 30,709 – and there were only 4,069 occupied houses.

Source A shows the number of people living at the large, comfortable houses on St James Street in the wealthy district of Westminster. Number 2 was home to a family of four and eight servants. At the same time, the census record for 3 Buck's Row in Whitechapel shows a family of two adults and eight children sharing one small house.

Lodging houses offered little more than a bed in dirty conditions.

- Some lodging houses had three eight-hour sleeping shifts a day, so beds could be used by the maximum number of people.
- The smell and heat in summer, and the huge number of rats, meant these lodging houses were truly awful.
- It is estimated that there were over 200 lodging houses in Whitechapel at this time, where more than 8,000 people – about a quarter of the local population – lived.

Key terms

Sanitation*

Conditions associated with public health, such as running water and sewerage systems.

Census*

A survey of everyone who lives in the country. It contains information such as their place of birth and occupation. They took place every 10 years from 1841, and are a useful source for historians.

Source A

Census record from 1881 for wealthy households in the West End.

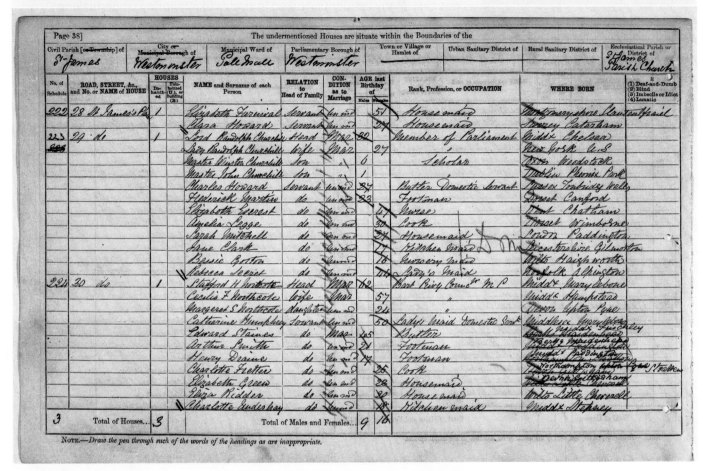

Model housing – the Peabody Estate

Whitechapel housing wasn't all bad. In 1875, parliament passed the Artisans' Dwellings Act in an attempt to improve the slums. In Whitechapel, a maze of narrow courtyards filled with cramped and unhealthy houses was replaced with 11 new blocks of flats. These were paid for by George Peabody, a wealthy American who had moved to London.

- The Peabody Estate opened in 1881 and provided 286 flats.
- Weekly rents started at a reasonable three shillings (15p) for a one-room flat and went up to six shillings (30p) for three rooms.
- The average weekly wage for a labourer at this time was 22 shillings and 6 pence (£1.12), and some poor working-class families spent as much as a third of this (8 shillings, or 40p, a week) on rent.

Exam-style question, Section A

Describe **two** features of working conditions in Whitechapel in the late 19th century.　　**4 marks**

Exam tip

For each feature identified, develop it with some supporting information.

Work in Whitechapel

Whitechapel's most famous factory was the Bell Foundry, where Big Ben was cast. Many residents worked in trades like tailoring, shoe-making and making matches. The work premises – known as sweatshops – were small, cramped and dusty, with little natural light. Hours were long (some sweatshop workers worked 20 hours a day and slept on-site) and wages were low.

Others worked in railway construction or as labourers in the London docks, where the amount of work on offer varied day to day leaving families with an uncertain income. Not everybody found work – the economy became severely depressed in the 1870s and unemployment was widespread.

Workhouses and orphanages

Source B

A photograph taken c1902, possibly to show a recent refurbishment at Whitechapel Workhouse. It shows a line of men waiting for admission to the 'tramps' ward.

Key term

Poor relief*

The system of giving benefits to the poor.

Workhouses had been set up earlier in the 19th century as part of the poor relief* system. They offered food and shelter to the very poor.

Inmates included the old, sick, disabled, orphans and unmarried mothers. Conditions were deliberately made worse to put poor people off from entering the workhouse except as a last resort.

- Inmates were expected to do hard manual labour and wear a uniform.
- Families were split up and could be punished even for trying to talk to each other.
- Vagrants, who stayed just one or two nights, were held separately from long-term residents, as they were thought to be lazy and a bad influence on the others.

Source C

A typical workhouse floor plan. South Grove workhouse in Whitechapel was based on this plan.

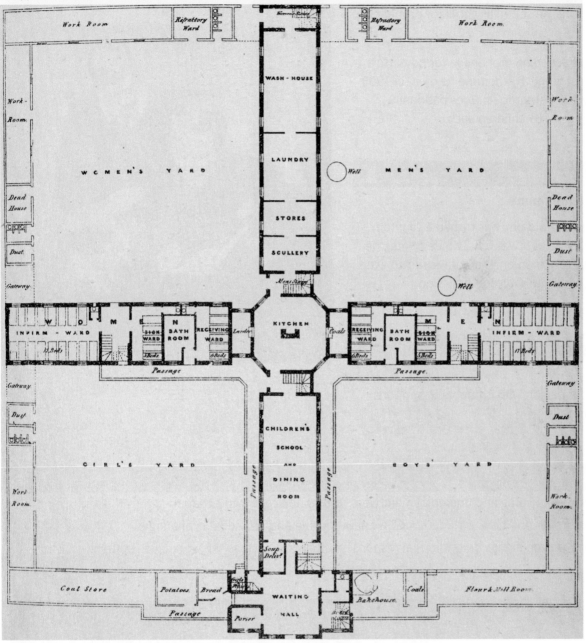

Activities

1 What can you learn from Source C about what workhouses were like?
2 What does Source D (see page 160) suggest about Thomas Barnardo?

Some people tried to do their best to help the poor. Dr Thomas Barnardo became heavily involved in the lives of poor children in Whitechapel. After seeing their living conditions, he set up a school for orphaned children.

In 1870, Barnardo opened an orphanage for boys. He later opened a girls' home. By the time he died, in 1905, there were nearly 100 Barnardo's homes nationally, caring for an average of 85 children each.

Extend your knowledge

Dr Barnardo's commitment

One night, an 11-year-old boy was turned away from Barnardo's orphanage as it was full. Two days later, he was found dead. From then on, the home's motto was: 'No Destitute* Child Ever Refused Admission'.

Key term

Destitute*

An extremely poor person who is unable to support themselves financially.

Source D

A photograph of Dr Thomas Barnardo, taken around 1870 to publicise his work.

Summary

- Poor housing, overcrowding and unemployment were commonplace in Whitechapel.
- Attempts to improve conditions included building new housing and providing orphanages.
- These solutions existed alongside traditional responses to poverty, such as the workhouse system.

Checkpoint

Strengthen

S1 Describe living conditions in a typical Whitechapel rookery.

S2 Explain why the Peabody Estate was created in Whitechapel.

Challenge

C1 Suggest two reasons why people living in Whitechapel found it difficult to lift themselves out of poverty.

C2 Why do you think many poor people would avoid going to the workhouse unless they absolutely had to?

How confident do you feel about your answers to these questions? Discuss your answers with other students and record your conclusions. Your teacher can give you some hints.

Immigration

Irish immigrants

The Irish population grew rapidly in the East End from the 1840s.

- The first immigrants were young men who came to London planning to travel on to America, but ran out of money before they could find a ship to take them there.
- They settled in areas near the river and made their living as 'navigators', or 'navvies' who did labouring jobs on canals, roads and railways, or as dockers on the River Thames.
- Many people thought that when they were drunk, Irish immigrants were often very violent.

Fenians

In the mid and late 19th century, Irish nationalists demanded freedom from rule by the UK.

- The fight was led by the Fenians, who were seen as a dangerous terrorist movement.
- After a bomb attack on Clerkenwell Prison, in December 1867, there was a huge surge of anti-Irish feeling.
- A new department of the Metropolitan Police, known as Special Branch, was formed to counter Irish terrorism.
- These events made life for Irish immigrants harder, as the press and many people saw all Irish people as possible traitors.

Source A

A drawing from the *Illustrated London News* (1862) showing Irish 'navvies' (navigators) building the Metropolitan Railway through East London.

Extend your knowledge

Dynamite Saturday

On a single day, 24 January 1885, the Fenians launched attacks on a number of central London landmarks. They included London Bridge, the House of Commons and the Tower of London – all powerful symbols of Britain. Journalists referred to this day as 'Dynamite Saturday'.

Eastern European Jewish immigrants

In the 1880s many Eastern European Jews arrived in Whitechapel, fleeing violence and persecution.

For security, as well as a shared culture and lower living costs, many Jewish immigrants chose to live together in Whitechapel. By 1888, although less than 1% of the population in Britain was Jewish, some areas of Whitechapel had a population that was 95% Jewish.

> ### Key terms
>
> **Anti-Semitic***
>
> Prejudiced against Jews.
>
> **Sabbath***
>
> A holy day each Saturday where Jews focus on worship.

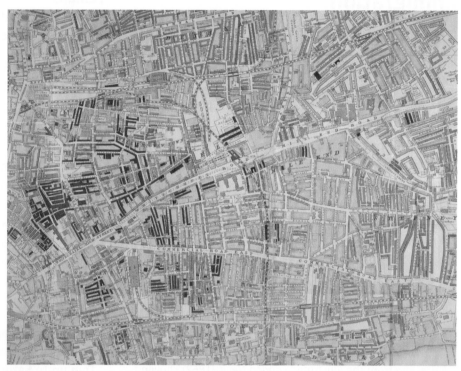

Figure 5.5 East London, showing Jewish settlement (blue) in the Spitalfields area of Whitechapel at the beginning of the 20th century.

Anti-Semitic* attitudes were common in Whitechapel. While resentment of Irish settlers was based on fear of the Fenians, resentment of Jewish settlers was based on cultural differences and stereotypes.

- The Jewish community faced hostility in Whitechapel as they seemed very different to native Londoners. Some immigrant Jews spoke a different language, Yiddish, and many locals were suspicious of their unfamiliar customs, such as the Jewish holy day of the Sabbath* celebrated each Saturday.

- Due to strict religious laws on diet and working days, Jews tended to live and work separately from other Londoners. This added to the suspicion against Jews in the community.

> ### Source B
>
> A report written by Charles Booth in 1889, entitled *Life and Labour of the People in London*. Booth was an English social researcher and reformer. He is famous for documenting working-class life in London.
>
> The newcomers have gradually replaced the English population in whole districts. They were formerly in Commercial Street. Now the Jews have flowed across the line; Hanbury Street, Fashion Street, Pelham Street, Booth Street, Old Montague Street, and they have taken over many streets and lanes and alleys. They fill whole blocks of model dwellings [like the Peabody Estate]; they have introduced new trades as well as new habits and they live and crowd together and work and go their own way independent of the great stream of London life surging around them.

- Jews were unfairly blamed for driving down wages as some of them were willing to accept low pay and long hours.
- Some newspapers at first claimed Jack the Ripper was Jewish. There was no evidence for this but it led to more hostility towards Jews.
- A small number of migrants from Eastern Europe, including Jews, became involved with anarchist and socialist organisations which were seen as dangerous by many people.

The growth of socialism and anarchism

Anarchists

- From the middle of the 19th century, radical political movements, such as Anarchism*, emerged across Europe. These groups wanted to overthrow governments.
- These movements were often treated harshly in countries such as France and Russia. Many of their leaders fled to London for safety.
- Some began to feel East London had become a safe haven for terrorists, and the police began to monitor their activities.
- Many people began to see anyone with an Eastern European accent as a terrorist. In reality, the threat they posed was exaggerated.

Source C

A photograph of the influential anarchist, Mikhail Bakunin, a Russian who encouraged anarchist worker's unions to fight for greater freedoms.

Socialists

- The Social Democratic Federation (SDF), the first socialist* party in Britain, was founded in 1881 to represent agricultural and industrial labourers, and the rights of women.
- Its leadership, sometimes known as Radicals, wanted a revolution to bring down the existing capitalist* system.
- The SDF was involved in the Trafalgar Square demonstration of 1887 that led to Bloody Sunday (see pages 144–149).
- They saw the police as only listening to the government and not caring about poor people.

Key term

Anarchism*

A political movement that opposes all forms of organised government.

Key terms

Socialist*

Someone who believes that poor people would get a better deal if the government nationalised (took over) important industries and services and ran them for the good of all – not for profit.

Capitalist*

Someone who believes individuals should be free to own property and businesses and make a profit.

The first ever elections to the newly-formed London County Council were in Autumn 1888. The SDF hoped to get elected in Whitechapel. Their campaign highlighted the stupidity of the police. This was very popular during the hunt for Jack the Ripper (see pages 173–183).

Rising tensions

- By 1888, the high unemployment and housing shortage in the East End focused national attention on immigration.
- Two parliamentary committees were formed to look into it. One of them investigated the sweatshop system, in which many workers were newly-arrived Jewish immigrants (see Source D).
- Sweatshops were illegal, but it was almost impossible for the police to deal with Eastern Europeans, as they spoke little English and the police spoke nothing but English (see Source E).
- As tension between immigrant and local populations increased, anti-semitic attitudes and beatings of Jews became common.
- On streets where both Eastern European and Irish immigrants mixed, tensions were particularly high, and the police considered them to be especially violent areas.

Source D

Evidence given to the House of Lords Committee on Sweated Trades in 1890, by Charles Freak, secretary of the Shoemaker Society, a trade union representing workers in the industry.

There is no feeling against these foreigners as foreigners. These Jew foreigners work in our trade at this common labour for 16 or 18 hours a day, and the consequence is that they make a lot of cheap and nasty stuff that destroys the market and injures us [because it is sold at such a low price]. The Jewish labourers cause the defeat of English workmen in their battle to attain higher wages. They do this by shameless blacklegging during disputes [working during strikes] and taking work out at any price.

Source E

From a memorandum by Superintendent Mulvaney of H Division, sent to Scotland Yard in 1904, suggesting his men should have lessons in Yiddish (a language spoken by Eastern European Jews).

Bills and circulars in this language are distributed and posted all over the division, but police know nothing of their purpose unless an interpreter is employed to translate them. As it is known that a number of these people are members of Continental Revolutionary Societies it would be very desirable to have members of the Service who could speak this language.

The Ripper murders made things even more tense.

- Anti-Jewish features in sensationalist* newspapers and journals like the *East London Observer* and the *Pall Mall Gazette* led to further harassment and street violence.
- Imaginary sketches of Jack the Ripper in local newspapers, like *Lloyd's Weekly News*, showed stereotyped* caricatures of Jews, with hooked noses, dark beards and dark felt hats.

People believed no Englishman could possibly have committed the Ripper murders so many people were convinced it must have been a Jew or an Irishman. During the Ripper investigation, Whitechapel was filled with police reinforcements aimed at preventing the outbreak of a full-scale anti-Jewish riot.

Key terms

Sensationalist*

Describing events in a deliberately exaggerated style to shock and impress.

Stereotyping*

Assuming all members of a group are alike – for example, looking similar, or having similar views.

Source F

Metropolitan Police H Division report by Superintendent Thomas Arnold, 6 November 1888.

On the morning of 30th Sept. last my attention was called to some writing on the wall [in] Goulston Sreet Whitechapel which consisted of the following words: "The Juwes are the men that will not be blamed for nothing." I knew that in consequence of a suspicion having fallen upon a Jew named 'John Pizer' alias 'Leather Apron' having committed a murder in Hanbury Street a short time previously, a strong feeling existed against the Jews generally. I was apprehensive [worried] that if the writing were left it would cause a riot. An Inspector was present with a sponge for the purpose of removing the writing when the Commissioner arrived on the scene.

Activities

1 Study Sources B, D and F. What can you learn from them about attitudes towards Jewish immigrants?

2 Study Source E. What can you learn from this about the problems the police faced in Whitechapel?

Summary

- By the 1880s, there had been two separate waves of recent immigration into the Whitechapel District: Irish and Eastern European.
- In both cases, there were fears that the immigrants brought with them dangerous political views.
- Immigration seemed to be a threat to local people's options for housing and jobs.
- Immigrant groups were likely to be stereotyped as dangerous criminals.

Checkpoint

Strengthen

S1 Give two reasons why Jewish and Irish immigration to London increased in the 19th century.

S2 Explain why there was hostility towards Irish immigrants in Whitechapel.

S3 Explain why there was hostility towards Eastern European immigrants in Whitechapel.

Challenge

C1 Explain why people were worried about political groups such as the Fenians, Anarchists and Socialists.

How confident do you feel about your answers to these questions? Reread the text and try again. Your teacher can give you some hints.

Evaluating usefulness: COAT method

When considering how useful a source is to a particular enquiry, first:

- **identify** content and try to link it to the enquiry to answer the question
- using that material, look carefully at the **provenance** of the source and consider how it affects the value of the source.

First, think about the content:

- Is what the content says typical of what others are saying about the topic?
- Does the author have some reason to give an unbalanced view of his or her content?

This will help show how useful the source is.

Consider the following when evaluating the content:

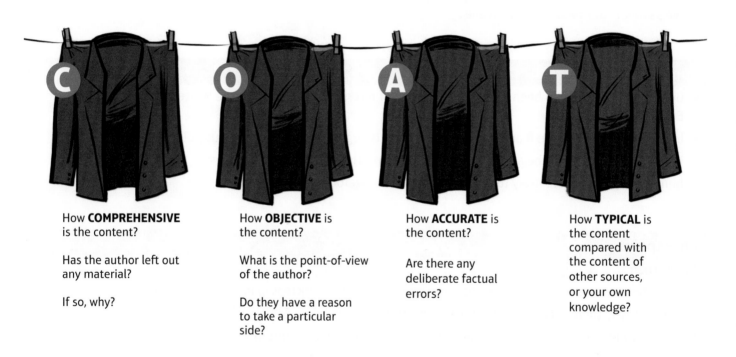

How **COMPREHENSIVE** is the content?

Has the author left out any material?

If so, why?

How **OBJECTIVE** is the content?

What is the point-of-view of the author?

Do they have a reason to take a particular side?

How **ACCURATE** is the content?

Are there any deliberate factual errors?

How **TYPICAL** is the content compared with the content of other sources, or your own knowledge?

Figure 5.6 The COAT method.

In summary, to work out how useful the content of a source is – put on your 'COAT'.

Consider this enquiry:

'How useful are Sources B and C (pages 162–163) for an enquiry into the problems encountered by the people of Whitechapel as a result of widespread immigration during the years 1881–90?'

Beginning with Source B, the material useful for the enquiry is:

1 'The newcomers have gradually replaced the English population in whole districts…'

2 '… they have taken over many streets and lanes and alleys. They fill whole blocks of model dwellings…'

3 '… they have introduced new trades as well as new habits…'

4 '… [they] go their own way independent of the great stream of London life…'

Is it comprehensive?	Is it objective?
The source looks at how Jewish people have taken over certain areas (1), including model dwellings (2), and have brought in new types of employment and lifestyles (3). It also suggests that Jews do not integrate with existing Londoners (4). But Jewish people worked very hard and brought lots of benefits, including boosting trade. This suggests the source to some extent gives the wrong impression of the new immigration.	The author has been selective in focusing on criticism, which is not a particularly objective approach. The author claims Jewish people took over large sections of the housing that had been built to improve the area at the expense of the existing residents.
Is it accurate?	**Is it typical?**
The source might exaggerate the amount of housing Jewish people took over. This might call into doubt the source's accuracy.	Does this reflect what other commentators wrote or said? How typical is the view taken by the author?

To write a good response about the usefulness of a source's content, you need an understanding of the circumstances in which the author was writing. This is called the historical context – the information given in Section 5.3. For example, you can use your knowledge to decide whether the content is exaggerated or accurate.

Finally, remember that to make a full evaluation of the usefulness of a source, you also need to consider its provenance.

Activity ?

With your teacher's guidance, try the COAT approach on Source C (page 163).

Learning outcome

- Understand the difficulties of policing the Whitechapel community.

Source A

Extract from *The Times* newspaper in 1853.

The professional policeman, clothed as such, exhibits the strength of a dozen rioters and paralyses opposition by the power that is felt to be at his back, the English law.

H Division

The Metropolitan Police force was split into 20 divisions, each responsible for a district of London and named with a letter of the alphabet. Whitechapel was covered by H Division.

The division was run by a superintendent and a chief inspector, with the support of 27 inspectors and 37 sergeants. The sergeants supervised around 500 ordinary officers, or constables, who went out on the beat.

There were also 15 detectives assigned to H Division from CID.

The work could be both boring and dangerous, and the pay was not very good. This meant that the standard of recruits was not always very high.

Police Constables (PCs) had to regularly meet with their beat sergeant and discuss what had happened so far. They would then record the conversation in their diary.

They would stop and question suspicious looking people.

Attitudes to the police were mixed. Some respected them as 'Bobbies' who helped to keep the peace. Others saw them as representatives of the government, and little more than violent thugs.

Constables would begin by marching out into Whitechapel with colleagues until they reached their 'beat' (area to patrol). They would then begin their patrol.

▶ An average beat constable's shift

Source B

A story published in *The Illustrated Police News*, 2 June 1883, about a gang attack on a Whitechapel policeman.

Savage Attack Upon A Policeman

John Harris, Jane Reynolds and Alfred Lindsey were charged in committing a murderous assault on Dennis Mortimer, a constable... Constable Mortimer heard loud cries of 'Stop him!' and as he tackled Harris a mob of young ruffians collected around him and commenced pelting him with stones and hitting him with sticks. Mortimer made strenuous efforts to protect himself, but on drawing his truncheon, according to a witness, the female Reynolds wrenched it from his hand and struck him on the side of the head with it, and another girl also hit him about the head. The prisoner and his gang made their escape, leaving the constable unconscious.

- However, many others had to work on the streets. Here they were vulnerable to attack and rape.
- As there was no contraception, many prostitutes were forced to have backstreet abortions. As a result many died.

Prostitution was a difficult issue for the police to manage. It was not illegal but was instead seen as a social problem that needed to be carefully monitored.

Alcohol

For many people living in Whitechapel, cheap, strong alcohol was the only escape they had from the terrible conditions they lived in. Alcoholism became a major problem. In just one mile (1.5 km) of the Whitechapel Road there were 45 pubs or gin palaces*, as well as a number of opium dens*. Drunken violence and crime created more problems for the police.

Policing Whitechapel

Whitechapel was a breeding ground for crime – from petty theft to murder. This made H Division's task particularly challenging. Many of the crimes were directly linked to the high levels of poverty and unemployment – people with no work would resort to crime rather than starve or go into the workhouse.

Prostitution

Many people in Victorian England had little sympathy for prostitutes. However, many women had no alternative if they needed to earn a living.

- Prostitution was not illegal in Victorian England, but was seen as a social problem.
- Prostitutes* lived difficult and dangerous lives.
- Some worked in brothels*. Others could afford to rent a room.

Key terms

Prostitute*

A person who offers sexual activity in return for payment.

Brothel*

A house where one or more prostitutes work.

Gin palace*

Extravagant, richly decorated gas-lit shop selling gin across a counter. Gin was a cheaply available, potent alcohol, popular with the poor. The light and splendour made a stark contrast with the dark, dirty streets.

Opium den*

A place where the drug opium was sold and smoked. Despite the name, the places could vary in appearance from an elegant bar room to a dark cellar.

Source C

A drawing in the *Illustrated Police News*, published on 2 June 1883. It accompanied the news report shown in Source B.

SAVAGE ATTACK ON A POLICEMAN.

The slums were a very difficult environment for the police to work in. The confined spaces, poor lighting and multiple entrances and exits meant there were always corners where criminals could hide.

Protection rackets

Some of the violence in Whitechapel was stirred up by gangs, some of which were made up of immigrants from Eastern Europe. These gangs demanded protection money from small business owners. Anyone who refused to pay had their shop or market stall smashed to pieces. The gangs also attacked each other.

Ordinary people were afraid to report gang members to the police. As such it was almost impossible to gather enough evidence to arrest gang members or put them on trial.

Because they were overstretched and understaffed, some areas of Whitechapel became 'no go' areas where the police made no attempt to stop criminal activities.

Police in the Whitechapel community

Police were not just expected to deal with crime.

They were also expected to deal with other social issues, such as: vagrancy, lunatics*, pubs, street traffic, sewage and litter, coinage, children, runaway horses, fires and accidents.

Key term

Lunatics*

In Victorian times this term was used to describe people with serious psychological disorders.

In 1867, the Metropolitan Streets Act was passed which even required all dogs to be muzzled. The police were expected to enforce this. This law was soon dropped as it was ignored by the public, including the well-off, respectable classes (Source D).

Some of these social work tasks brought the police into immediate conflict with Whitechapel residents.

- Their poor relief work linked them to the workhouse, and made people very hostile to them.
- Attempts to control prostitution were resented by women whose lives depended on earning enough to escape starvation.

On the other hand, the poor people of Whitechapel could see that H Division also provided real benefits: hosting soup kitchens (often to try to get information from witnesses, as the Home Office preferred not to offer money); looking after stray children; and stopping runaway horses.

Most people felt that a police force was necessary – they just didn't like their methods or priorities.

Activity   **?**

What can you infer from Sources C and D about the difficulties the police faced in Whitechapel?

Source D

A cartoon published in *Fun* magazine, 15 August 1868. *Fun* was a weekly magazine aimed at well-educated readers.

DOG AND DODGE.

Policeman :—"You must put that dog's muzzle on, sir!"

Wide-awake Party :—"Excuse me, Robert, you're mistaken. The order is that no dog shall be allowed in the streets *without* a muzzle. As you perceive, he has got a muzzle, but prefers carrying it!"

As the police were expected to enforce so many laws, they were sometimes seen as interfering busybodies, who should focus more on catching criminals.

Overall, poor people needed the police to defend them, and because they were figures of authority, they were able to do this.

However, the fact that policemen were in authority was also the reason they were resented, as people did not like being told what to do in their everyday lives.

Activity

Roleplay a conversation between two residents of Whitechapel about the police of the time. Try to focus on the positive and negative views of their work.

Summary

- Police were often seen as the government in uniform. This made them unpopular and there were many physical attacks on them.
- Prostitution, alcoholism and the physical layout of the narrow streets gave the police particular challenges.
- Police numbers were too few to cope with lawlessness, so some rougher areas were left without police supervision.
- Many people believed the police were too concerned with enforcing regulations at the expense of preventing serious crime.

Checkpoint

Strengthen

S1 Make a list of all the different problems the police faced when trying to enforce the law.

S2 Give two examples of laws that policemen were expected to enforce.

Challenge

C1 Using the sources and information in this section as a prompt, write a diary entry from a policeman in the 1880s describing a typical 'beat'.

How confident do you feel about your answers to these questions? If you are unsure, go back to the text and reread the sources to find the evidence you need.

5.5 Investigative policing in Whitechapel

Learning outcomes

- Understand the problems posed for H Division by both the media and their rivalry with the City of London police, during the investigation of the Jack the Ripper murders.
- Know about the detective techniques used in the investigation.
- Understand how investigative methods changed as a result of the Ripper case.

The Jack the Ripper murders

In 1888, five women were murdered in and around Whitechapel. The victims were:

- Mary Ann Nichols, found in Buck's Row on 31 August
- Annie Chapman, found in the back yard of 29 Hanbury Street, Spitalfields, on 8 September
- Elizabeth Stride, found in Berners Street on 30 September
- Catherine Eddowes, found in Mitre Square, Aldgate, also on 30 September
- Mary Jane Kelly, found inside 13 Miller's Court, Dorset Street, Spitalfields on 9 November.

The police believed that all had been killed by the same person. The murderer was never caught but has been given the popular nickname 'Jack the Ripper'.

The police investigation into the murders gives us an insight into both the methods used by the police at the time, and the challenges they faced.

Source A

A drawing from *Famous Crimes Past and Present*, 1903. PC Neil discovers Mary Ann Nichols's body in Buck's Row.

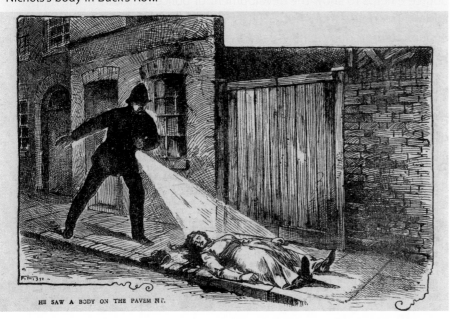

HE SAW A BODY ON THE PAVEMENT.

Source B

An inquest sketch of the body of Catherine Eddowes by Frederick William Foster, showing details of extensive mutilation. Sketches were often used to illustrate the methods of violent criminals and to link incidents to previous murders.

Source C

A letter sent on 27 September 1888 to the Central News Agency was at first believed to be a hoax but was later reproduced on this poster, which appeals to the general public for information.

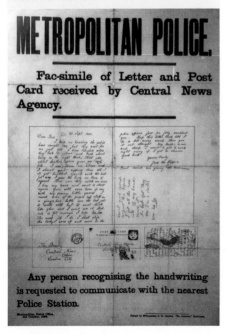

The problem of police and the media

Inspector Frederick Abberline and his CID team led the Jack the Ripper case, working with the uniformed men of H Division.

Almost immediately, their task was made much harder by more than 300 letters and postcards sent to them, or to the newspapers, by men claiming to be the murderer.

Source C helps to show the development of police methods in the Ripper inquiry. The police thought this letter (addressed 'Dear Boss') important enough to reproduce in newspapers and wall posters, hoping someone would recognise the handwriting.

The problem of police force rivalry

A short time after the discovery of Catherine Eddowes's body, PC Alfred Long of H Division discovered an important clue on Goulston Street, half a mile away.

It was a piece of Eddowes's apron, smeared with blood and faeces (human waste). In the alleyway behind, there was a message scrawled in chalk on the wall: 'The Juwes are the men that will not be blamed for nothing'.

Source D

A newspaper image from the *Illustrated Police News*, published 13 October 1888. It shows a local resident and street trader, Louis Diemshutz, finding Elizabeth Stride's body.

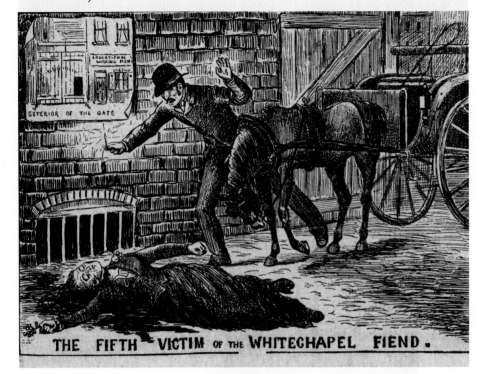

Extend your knowledge

Murderous 1880s?

In 1888, 122 cases of violent death were recorded in London: 28 were classed as murder, and the rest as manslaughter. The population of Greater London in the 1880s was approximately five and a half million.

In 2013, when the population of Greater London was around seven million, there were 113 reported murders. However, just ten years earlier, in 2003, the murder rate was double that. So, murder rates in the capital are very variable, and it's difficult to say if 1888 was a particularly bad year.

Commissioner Warren ordered the message to be washed off before it could be photographed – apparently fearing a backlash against the Jewish community. But he may also have had another motive.

Eddowes was killed inside the boundaries of the City of London, which had its own police force, independent of the Met, and it is possible he did not want to be beaten to the capture of the serial killer by a rival force. This bitter rivalry between the forces was one of the biggest problems for police investigation in and around Whitechapel.

Activities   ?

1 Study Sources A and D. What issues might there be with using drawings like this as evidence?

2 Study Source C. What can you learn from this about how the police attempted to catch Jack the Ripper?

The police investigation – developing techniques

In the early stages of the investigation, after the discovery of Mary Ann Nichols's body on 31 August, the police used the following methods in their inquiry:

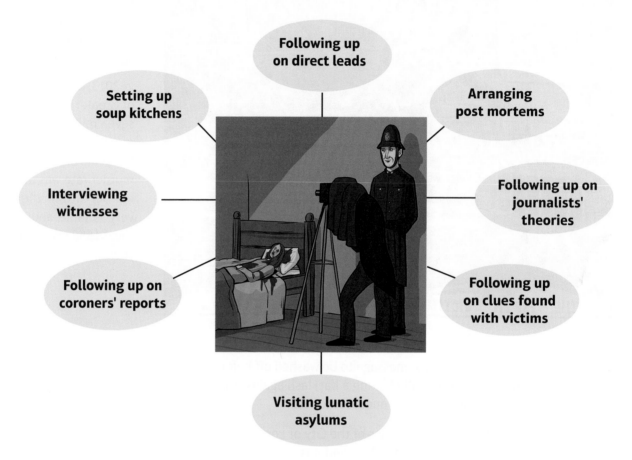

Figure 5.7 Investigative methods during the Ripper inquiry.

- **Following up direct leads from the public:** The public suggested leads to the police, but they were frequently unhelpful and wasted police time.

- **Using evidence from post mortems*:** A local doctor suggested that the cut marks on one of the victims indicated the killer was left-handed and must have some knowledge of anatomy* and possibly experience of dissection*. For many weeks, inquiries were made at slaughterhouses and hospitals.

- **Following up indirect leads from articles by investigating journalists:** One example of this was the police follow-up on a report in the *Manchester Guardian*. The report suggested the murderer could be a local man, nicknamed 'Leather Apron'. 'Leather Apron' was later identified as John Pizer, who had solid alibis* for the time of Nichols's murder and Annie Chapman's a week later.

- **Following up on clues in the victims' possessions:** A fragment of an envelope found near Annie Chapman's body contained the seal of the Sussex Regiment. It was discovered these seals could be bought in many post offices and so could not be used to identify a suspect. Officers also visited several pawnbrokers and jewellers shops to try to track down the rings missing from Annie's fingers.

- **Visiting lunatic asylums*:** Because the murders were so savage, it was assumed that the Ripper was insane, and could have escaped from an asylum, or been housed in one after his crimes.

- **Following up on coroners' reports:** Dr Wynne Baxter suggested a theory about the skills and motive of the murderer (Source F), which was challenged by detectives investigating later murders (Source G).

- **Interviewing key witnesses:** Very few reliable eye-witnesses actually saw the events surrounding the murders. However, Elizabeth Long claimed to have seen a man talking to Annie Chapman a few minutes before she was discovered dead. Police ignored her evidence because it conflicted with the doctor's report about the time of death.

- **Setting up soup kitchens:** The Met were not allowed to offer money as a reward, as it might attract time-wasters, but local police encouraged poor people to come forward as witnesses by promising a hot meal.

Key terms

Alibi*
Proof that an accused person was in some other place at the time a crime was committed.

Lunatic asylum*
The Victorian term for a psychiatric hospital.

Source E

A poster displayed by the police in September 1888.

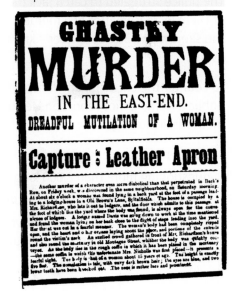

Source F

From the coroner's report of Dr Wynne Baxter into the murder of Annie Chapman, 14 September 1888.

The injuries had been made by someone who had considerable anatomical skill and knowledge. There were no meaningless cuts. The organ [Chapman's womb] had been taken by one who knew where to find it. No unskilled person could have known this or have recognised it when found. For instance, no mere slaughterer of animals could have carried out these operations. It must have been someone accustomed to the post mortem room with a desire to possess the missing organ.

Following Dr Baxter's coroner's report on the death of Annie Chapman in September (Source F), the police became more interested in investigating hospitals and veterinary surgeons. However, the attack on Catherine Eddowes was savage, but clumsy, and cast doubt on the killer's skill (Source G). As a result, police began questioning butchers instead.

Source G

From a report by Chief Inspector Swanson into the murder of Kate Eddowes, 6 November 1888.

There is no evidence of anatomical knowledge that suggested the killer was a qualified surgeon, otherwise the Police could have narrowed their enquiries down to certain classes of persons. On the other hand, as in the Metropolitan Police cases, the medical evidence showed that the murder could have been committed by a hunter, a butcher, a slaughterman, as well as a student in surgery or a properly qualified surgeon.

The police struggled to catch Jack the Ripper. Criticism of them increased after two murders took place on the same night, 30 September – known as the 'Double Event'.

To counter the criticism, Chief Inspector Swanson made public a Home Office report on Metropolitan Police methods, including:

- house-to-house searches
- questioning more than 2,000 lodging house residents
- distributing 80,000 handbills (Source J)
- getting help from the Thames River Police to question sailors in the docks, and neighbouring divisions of the Met to search opium dens.

Source H

The recollections of Inspector Frederick Abberline, reported in the *Pall Mall Gazette*, 24 March 1903.

I gave myself up to the study of the cases. Many a time, even after we had carried our inquiries as far as we could – and we made no fewer than 1,600 sets of papers about our investigations – instead of going home when I was off duty, I used to patrol the district until four or five o'clock in the morning. While keeping my eyes wide open for clues of any kind, many and many a time I gave those wretched, homeless women, who were Jack the Ripper's special prey, fourpence or sixpence for a shelter to get them away from the streets and out of harm's way.

Source I

From a report in the *East London Advertiser* newspaper, published 15 September 1888. The writer is commenting on Metropolitan Police Commissioner, Sir Charles Warren's decision to bring in soldiers to help police in Whitechapel.

The double stupidity of weakening his detective force and strengthening his ordinary police force from reserves and the military destroys two safeguards of a community. It deprives it of a specially trained force of men with brainpower specially adapted for detective work and it takes away the old community constable, to be replaced by a man with a few years' military service, but with no other qualification for serving the public. Nothing has indeed been more characteristic of the hunt for the Whitechapel murderer than the lack of local knowledge displayed by the police. They seem to know little of the dark alleyways of the neighbourhood and still less of the bad characters who swarm through them.

Activities ?

1. Study Source E. What does it tell you about how the police tried to find information about the killer?

2. Study Sources F and G. In what ways do these two sources disagree about the likely identity of Jack the Ripper?

3. Study Source H. Suggest two reasons why this might be useful as evidence about the methods the police used in the Ripper investigation.

As well as criticising police methods the press made the investigation more difficult by publishing rumours, interviews with unreliable witnesses, and by suggesting the suspect was 'foreign'. The police had to follow up on these stories, wasting valuable time.

Investigative methods became increasingly bizarre. Some policemen adopted disguises: there were reports of men dressed as prostitutes to lure the Ripper into a trap – though they apparently refused to remove their moustaches! Some wore strips of rubber attached to their boots hoping to sneak up quietly on the murderer.

The police also experimented with bloodhounds. The dogs, Barnaby and Burgho, performed well in tracking trials in London parks, but the police failed to pay their owner who then refused to work further with the police.

Source J

Handbill distributed by the Metropolitan Police, 30 September 1888.

POLICE NOTICE.

TO THE OCCUPIER.

On the mornings of Friday, 31st August, Saturday 8th, and Sunday, 30th September, 1888, Women were murdered in or near Whitechapel, supposed by some one residing in the immediate neighbourhood. Should you know of any person to whom suspicion is attached, you are earnestly requested to communicate at once with the nearest Police Station.

Metropolitan Police Office,
30th September, 1888.

Printed by M'Corquodale & Co. Limited, " The Armoury," Southwark.

Source K

A sketch for the *East London Observer*, 13 October 1888, on the training of bloodhounds.

SIR CHARLES WARREN'S NEW CRIMINAL TRACKERS: MR. BROUGH'S BLOODHOUNDS BEING TRAINED.

Obstacles to police success

Lack of forensic techniques

Compared to modern police forces, the Met had almost no scientific forensic* techniques to help them. Their only hope, it seemed, was to catch the killer in the act. Without basic forensic techniques their chances of success were severely limited:

- It would be another 12 years or so before fingerprinting was used to detect criminals.
- DNA evidence only began to be used in the later part of the 20th century.
- Scientists could not yet detect the difference between animal and human blood – let alone blood groups.
- There would eventually be a useful database of criminals' mug shots* at Scotland Yard, but this was not yet large enough to be effective.
- Crime scene photography was not yet common. The police only photographed one of the crime scenes.

Key terms

Forensic*

Using scientific methods and techniques to investigate crime.

Mug shot*

A head-and-shoulders photograph, typically taken of a person after arrest.

The Vigilance Committee

Some people were so frustrated by the police's failure to catch the killer that they took matters into their own hands. On 10 September, a group of businessmen and traders set up the Whitechapel Vigilance Committee.

Their aims were:

- to offer rewards for information that led to the killer's arrest
- to patrol the streets, making as much noise as possible, in the hope of catching the Ripper.

The Home Secretary refused to offer a reward as he believed it would encourage time wasters. The police were sent over 300 hoax letters, suggesting he was right.

The actions of the Vigilance Committee disrupted the police investigation. Some of the Committee may have had grudges against the police and wanted to make them look incompetent.

Exam-style question, Section A

Study Sources F and L

How useful are Sources F and L for an enquiry into the difficulties the police faced in trying to capture the East End serial murderer? **8 marks**

Exam tip

For each source, make sure that you develop your answer by testing how **comprehensive**, how **objective**, how **accurate** and how **typical** they are (COAT). In doing this, include some of your own contextual knowledge. Show also how the provenance of each source affects its usefulness.

Extend your knowledge

Royal intervention

Queen Victoria intervened personally in the Ripper investigation, sending two telegrams with practical advice. She said dark passageways should be lit, the murderer's clothes should be found and cattle and passenger ships should be searched. Her interest led to rumours that the royal family was involved in the case.

The police investigation – lessons learnt and improvements to 1900

Improvements in technique – the Bertillon System

The failure to catch the Ripper led to a review of police record-keeping. The Bertillon System (see Source L) was introduced to the Met in 1894. Measurements of suspects were taken, their mug shots captured, and records stored in a central file. These unique identifiers could be used to catch repeat criminals, but there is not much evidence of their successful use by the CID.

Physical measurements began to be replaced by fingerprint records during the following decade, but Bertillon's photographic methods are still used today.

Source L

From Bertillon's book *Identification Anthropométrique* (1893), explaining a system for taking measurements of suspects.

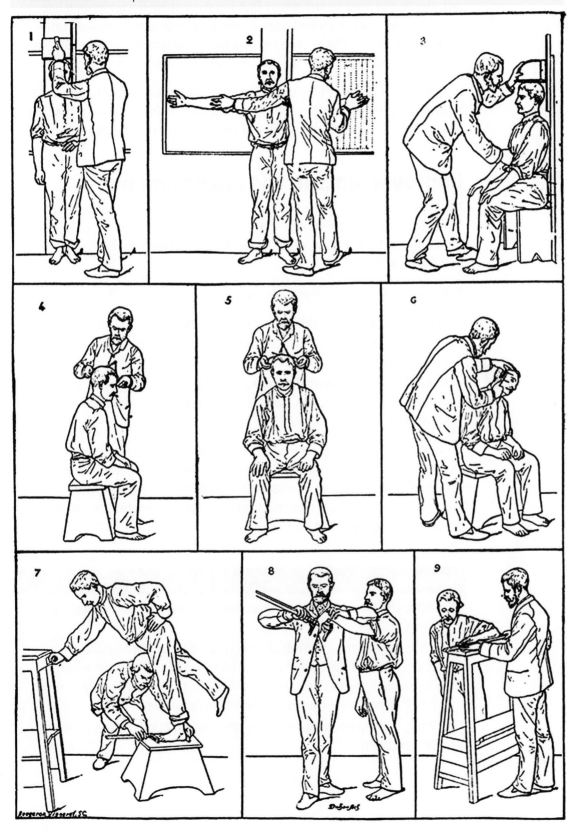

Improvements in communication

In 1888, police could only communicate from a distance by using a whistle. By the end of the century, the Met were beginning to benefit from the introduction of telephone lines. H Division did not have a telephone line until 1901, and only installed a telephone exchange in their police station in 1907. Similarly, although the Kent Police introduced bicycles in 1896, and most rural forces had them by 1905, H Division waited until 1909.

In summary, it is doubtful whether the great public outcry at the time of the Ripper murders had much overall impact on improving detection. That had to wait for the scientific discoveries of the early years of the 20th century.

Improvements in the environment

The Whitechapel murders led to a change in thinking about the causes of crime. Some in the government started to see a link between poor living conditions and crime. Laws were passed to begin to improve health and housing conditions.

The murders led to two important laws:

- **The Houses of the Working Classes Act (1890)** allowed the new London County Council to begin housing development schemes to replace slums with mass low-cost housing.
- **The Public Health Amendment Act (1890)** gave more powers to local councils to improve toilets, paving, rubbish collection and other sanitary* services.

However, it was not all good news. Though there were no more serial killings, murders continued to occur regularly in the 1890s. More immediately, hooliganism increased, as youths, pretending to be Jack the Ripper, frightened women. There was more violence against prostitutes and an increase in burglary in the early 1890s.

Key terms

Sanitary*

Relating to conditions that affect health and cleanliness, such as the supply of clean drinking water.

Activities ?

1 What else could the police have done to catch Jack the Ripper, given the resources at the time?

2 Make a list of the methods that were used by the Metropolitan Police to try to arrest the East End serial killer in 1888. Divide them into methods that you think were sensible and those that you think were not. Compare your list with a partner. Do you agree?

3 What role did newspapers play in the investigations? Were they a help or a problem?

Summary

- The failure to deal with the Ripper murders in 1888 led to enormous criticism of H Division, the Metropolitan Police and the CID team at Scotland Yard.
- Police methods were inadequate, but criticism was often unfair and paid no attention to the huge difficulties the police faced during the investigation.
- Some lines of inquiry by the CID in 1888 were imaginative and resourceful, given their lack of scientific knowledge compared with modern day police forces.
- The Metropolitan Police were slow to learn the lessons of the failed Ripper investigation, and improvements in detection were modest up to 1900.
- There were considerable improvements in lighting, housing and health – all as a direct result of national concern about the East End serial killings.

Checkpoint

Strengthen

S1 Look at Sources B–E. Make a mind map of the methods the police used to try to catch the Ripper in each case.

S2 Suggest one reason why the Vigilance Committee made it more difficult to catch the killer.

S3 Suggest two ways in which the Ripper murders led to better living conditions in Whitechapel.

Challenge

C1 Look at the difficulties the police faced in their Ripper enquiries. Which of these obstacles do you think was the most damaging to the police investigation? Explain your answer.

How confident do you feel about your answers to these questions? If you are unsure, form a group with other students, discuss the answers and then record your conclusions. Your teacher can give you some hints.

Asking questions: Whitechapel workhouse

Historians ask themselves three sorts of questions:

- content
- provenance
- context.

Look at Source A.

Source A

A sketch showing residents of the Whitechapel workhouse at Christmas 1874.

CHRISTMAS IN THE WHITECHAPEL WORKHOUSE,

Content questions: What are you looking at? You have some important help from the caption, but even without that, you can see Source A shows the residents of some kind of communal home at Christmas.

Provenance questions: Now you need the caption! Remember, for provenance, you need to break things down into nature, origin and purpose.

- Nature – it's an artist's sketch.
- Origin comes from the caption – this was drawn, possibly at the Whitechapel workhouse, and possibly from memory, during the festive season in 1874.
- Purpose can be hard for a drawing such as this. Does it look like it was set up specially? Might it be used as propaganda? In this case, it is fairly easy to think of a propaganda purpose. Perhaps it was drawn to make the point that workhouses genuinely did look after poor Londoners.

Context questions: You know several things that are relevant to Source A, including the following:

- The idea of the workhouse was that conditions should be worse than those that could be provided by a labourer for his family.
- Among residents of workhouses were the old, sick, disabled, orphans and unmarried mothers.
- Because the residents were made to wear a uniform they felt humiliated.

So, if you were asked how useful Source A is as evidence about conditions in the workhouse, you could say something like this, covering content, provenance and context:

'Source A is only partially useful as evidence about the conditions in workhouses. It shows a positive scene of poor people being looked after at Christmas, however we know it wasn't always like this as workhouses were designed to be unpleasant. It's possible the source was made to paint the workhouses in a positive light, making it less useful.'

What this does (and what you can do) is explain why the source is useful, using criteria based on the three types of question.

Activities ?

1. In small groups, study Source C (page 185). How useful is this source as evidence about the conditions in workhouses? Answer this big question by answering the following smaller questions:

   a content questions

   b provenance questions

   c context questions.

2. Compare your answers with others. You probably came up with some different answers. Does this mean one group has to be wrong?

Source B

From the novel *Captain Lobe* by Margaret Harkness, published in 1889. It features the new Whitechapel workhouse at South Grove.

The Whitechapel Union is a model workhouse; that is to say, it is the very purpose of the Poor Law made into stone and brick. The men are not allowed to smoke in it; the young women never taste tea, and the old ones may not have a cup during the long afternoons, only at half-past six o'clock morning and night, when they also receive a small hunch of bread with butter scraped over the surface, which is so dear to their hearts as well as their stomachs. The young people never go out, never see a visitor, and the old ones only get one holiday in the month. Then the aged poor people may be seen skipping like lambs outside the doors of this prison, while they jabber to their friends and relations. A little gruel morning and night, meat twice a week, that is the food of the grown-up people, seasoned with hard work and prison discipline. What shall we say of the woman, or man, hurt by misfortune, who must come there or die in the street? Why should old people be punished for their existence?

Source C

A photograph taken in the women's ward of Whitechapel workhouse infirmary in 1902.

The **content** of Source B is fairly easy to understand, but the **provenance** makes it a little more difficult to **assess**. Although you might think it is a factual account of life in the workhouse, it is written in a novel, and is fictional. It is likely to be based on the author's experiences, but we cannot be sure it represents the true nature of South Grove workhouse.

Source C, on the other hand, is a photograph, preserving a moment in time from the past. We don't know all we might like to about its **origin**, but – since it is taken in the workhouse and its **purpose** is probably to show that conditions there are very good for sick people – this helps us to gain an understanding of workhouse life. We must be **cautious**, however, as such photographs were often set up to show life at its best.

One thing Source C does not tell you is how many people were living in the infirmary. There is a reason for this. Those who were in charge of workhouses such as South Grove, knew that living conditions were overcrowded, and they may not have wanted to have criticisms like those in Source D.

Source D

From a survey of all London's workhouse infirmaries conducted in 1866 by the Poor Law Board. The Board consisted of elected officials who reported on conditions in workhouses in their areas. These comments are about the Whitechapel workhouse.

- Ventilation was inadequate and there was a problem with the drains in the male imbeciles' basement [where people with psychiatric illnesses were housed].
- There were insufficient nursing staff and the medical officers were overworked and underpaid.
- There was very little furniture in the sick wards other than the beds.
- The beds were inadequate in several respects.
- Only three roller towels a week were provided for a large ward, together with a pound of soap which was also used to wash the furniture. A single comb per ward was provided.
- The general sick had no games although dominoes were provided for the imbeciles.
- A separate ward for sick children should be provided.
- The labour ward should be moved so that screams could not be heard in adjacent wards.

All four of these sources are only partially useful for answering the big question – what were conditions really like in the workhouses?

So the historian looks for another source: for example, records about workhouses at the National Archive. This adds detail: the age, gender and health of residents of the Whitechapel workhouse at this time, including lots of letters written by those who were in charge.

This leads to another question: was this a typical Victorian workhouse? So historians then compare the records for Whitechapel with other workhouses run by Poor Law administrators.

Asking questions in the exam

The exam gives you a start by asking questions. The best way to do well is to ask some more questions – to establish the criteria you will use to make and explain your judgements, and to help you work out the best answers. The criteria you use as the reasons for your answer are one of the main things you will get marks for. So:

- ask yourself the questions
- use the questions to help you decide the best criteria
- use the criteria to explain your answer.

Activities ?

1 Look at the provenance of Source D. What might be a particular strength of this source as evidence about workhouse conditions?

2 Now look at Source E. It was drawn for inclusion in a local newspaper. How much value would a source like this have for the enquiry?

THINKING HISTORICALLY Evidence (3a)

The value of evidence

Look at Source B, then work through the tasks that follow.

1 Write down at least two ways in which the account is useful for explaining what conditions were like at South Grove.

2 Compare your answers with a partner, then try to come up with at least one limitation of the source for explaining what conditions were like at South Grove.

3 With your partner, decide how useful this source is for explaining the experiences of all residents at South Grove on a scale of 1 to 10 (10 being very useful).

4 What if the source was used to answer the question: 'How were young people cared for at South Grove?'

   a Write down any ways in which the source is useful for answering this new question.

   b Write down any limitations for answering the new question.

   c Can you think of another enquiry about the South Grove workhouse for which this would be a useful source? Write it down and score the source on a scale of 1 to 10.

5 Compare your scores out of 10. How does the question being asked affect how useful a source is? Explain your answer.

6 Can you think of any other factors that might affect the usefulness of the source?

Local newspapers

Source E shows you some of the strengths and weaknesses of local newspapers as sources. The illustration shows a child escaping from the St Giles workhouse, not far from South Grove. Most national newspapers would focus on workhouse conditions in general; but, in a local newspaper, just about everybody who read it must have known that particular workhouse. A local newspaper shows the effects of unusual stories in a single area, and gives us insights into normal life. This account would certainly back up the experiences written in Margaret Harkness's novel (Source B), but might not be typical of workhouses as a whole.

Source E

A sketch from the *Illustrated Police News* (1882). It shows a boy escaping from a local workhouse.

Using the range of sources

In the examination, you are asked to suggest a possible question and a type of source that you could use to follow up another source. As an example, this is what you might do if asked this about Source D. The framework of the question helps you through the four-stage process.

a The detail you might follow up could be one of the problems listed, e.g. shortage of nursing staff.

b The question you might ask is: 'How common were shortages of… ?'

c There are lots of different types of source in this unit. You could suggest any one of these:

- Evidence presented to parliament committees
- Local newspapers
- Official records of employment in workhouses.

d Lastly, you have to explain the reason for your choice:

- Parliamentary committee reports (because, if it was common, politicians and experts would probably write down the evidence before suggesting new laws to regulate workhouses).
- Local newspapers (because, if this survey was reported in a Whitechapel newspaper, such cases would probably always be written about, so you would see if there were other reports elsewhere).
- Official records (because Poor Law boards will have records, including lists of all the problems and suggestions for how these could be solved).

Activities ?

Using the range of sources

How useful a source is depends on the question being asked. Look at all of the sources in this chapter, and then decide which sources would be most useful to answer the following enquiry questions:

1 Why did the police find it difficult to control public demonstrations?

2 What was housing like in Whitechapel?

3 Why was there so much tension between East Enders and immigrants in the 1880s?

4 Why was it so difficult for the police to catch Jack the Ripper?

5 What problems were faced by policemen on the beat?

Recap: Whitechapel, c1870–c1900: Crime, policing and the inner city

There are three questions in this section of the exam paper. This recap section is structured around the demands of the three questions.

- The **Two features quiz** is designed to help you prepare for the first question, which requires you to remember details about a topic in this section of the course. However, you'll need to use your knowledge to interpret the sources and answer the questions linked to them

- The **This source is useful for...** table helps you prepare for the second question in the exam, which gives you two sources and asks you how useful they would be for a particular enquiry.*

- The **All about the details** activity helps you think about the types of source and how they can be used for new enquiries.

- Finally, the **Advantages and disadvantages of particular types of evidence** table helps to assess their strengths and weaknesses.

Two features quiz

For each topic below, list as many facts or features as you can. Aim to have at least two features for every topic.

1 Bloody Sunday, 1887
2 Whitechapel's 'rookeries'
3 'Model' dwellings
4 'Sweated' trades
5 'Unfortunates'
6 Workhouses
7 Dr Thomas Barnardo
8 Irish 'navvies'
9 Fenians
10 The Whitechapel Vigilance Committee

11 The work of Charles Booth
12 'Leather Apron'
13 *The Illustrated Police News*
14 Anarchists
15 The 'Dear Boss' Letter, 1888
16 The 'Double Event', 1888
17 The Bertillon System
18 The Social Democratic Federation
19 'Penny dreadfuls'
20 Local watch committees

This source is useful for...
Copy and complete the table.

Sources	Enquiry	Historical context	One way the source is useful and one way it is not useful
5.1 A (page 151) and D (page 153)	Did crime rates go down in the late 19th century?	Some historians have suggested that improving police forces led to lower crime rates.	Source A is useful because it shows official government figures that show offences were below average in the late 1870s, but you cannot tell if this is typical of the whole period of the enquiry. Source D describes the difficulties with gathering correct statistics, but it does tell us that the police were careful to compile accurate records.
5.5 K (page 179)		The Metropolitan Police tried some unusual techniques in the Ripper investigation.	

All about the details

Copy and complete the table.

Source	Detail	Question I would ask	Type of source I would use	How this might help answer my question
5.1 F (page 154)	Leading opposition politicians, opposed to the present government, have used these riots to their own advantage by shamefully supporting the mob.	*Did opposition politicians support the mob?*	*Records of debates in parliament.*	*Parliament would record what opposition MPs were saying.*
5.3 D (page 164)				

Advantages and disadvantages of particular types of evidence

Copy and complete the table.

Type of source	Advantages	Disadvantages
Memoirs of policemen		*They may give a justification of their own actions. They may not recall events from long ago accurately.*
Records of the local court	*They are official documents detailing evidence from witnesses for both prosecution and defence.*	
H Division police station records		
Home Office statistics		
Newspapers		

Preparing for your GCSE Paper 1 exam

Paper 1 overview

Your Paper 1 is in two sections that examine the Historic Environment and the Thematic Study. Together they count for 30% of your History assessment. The questions on the Historic Environment: Whitechapel, c1870–c1900: crime, policing and the inner city are in Section A and are worth 10% of your History assessment. Allow about a third of the examination time for Section A, making sure you leave enough time for Section B.

History Paper 1	Historic Environment and Thematic Depth Study			Time 1 hour 15 minutes
Section A	Historic Environment	Answer 3 questions	16 marks	25 mins
Section B	Thematic Study	Answer 3 questions	32 marks + 4 SPaG marks	50 mins

Historic Environment: Whitechapel, c1870–c1900: crime, policing and the inner city

You will answer Question 1 and Question 2, which is in two parts.

Q1 Describe two features of... (4 marks)

You are given a few lines to write about each feature. Allow five minutes to write your answer. It is only worth four marks, so keep the answer brief.

Q2(a) How useful are Sources A and B... (8 marks)

You are given two sources to make judgements about. They are in a separate sources booklet, so you can keep them in front of you while you write your answer. Allow 15 minutes for this question, to give yourself time to read both sources carefully. Make sure your answer refers to both sources.

You should **ask yourself the following questions about** the sources:

- What useful information do they give? What do they say or show? Check the question and only give details that are directly relevant to that topic.
- What can you infer? What do they suggest?

You must also **evaluate** the sources.

- Use contextual knowledge – for example, to evaluate accuracy or how typical they are.
- Use the provenance (nature, origin, purpose of the source) to weigh up the strengths and limitations of each source.
- Make **judgements** about the usefulness of each source, giving clear reasons. These should be based on the accuracy of the content, judged against your knowledge, and the provenance of the source.

Analyse	Evaluate
• *Useful information* • *What does it suggest?*	• *Contextual knowledge* • *Its strengths and limitations*

Q2(b) Study Source ... How could you follow up Source ... to find out more about...? (4 marks)

You are given a table to complete when you answer this question. It has four parts to it:

- the detail you would follow up
- the question you would ask
- the type of source you could use to find the information
- your explanation of how this information would help answer the question.

Allow five minutes to write your answer. You should keep your answer brief and not try to fill extra lines. The question is only worth four marks. Plan your answer so that all the parts link. Your answer will not be strong if you choose a detail to follow up, but then cannot think of a question or type of source that would help you follow it up.

Paper 1, Question 1

Describe **two** features of 'model' dwellings in the Whitechapel district in the late 19th century.
(4 marks)

Exam tip

Keep your answer brief. Two points with some extra information about each of them.

Basic answer

Feature 1:
Model dwellings were new houses designed in the 1870s.
Feature 2:
Model dwellings replaced slums.

The answer has identified two features, but with no supporting information.

Verdict

This is a basic answer because two valid features are given, but there is no supporting information.
Use the feedback to re-write this answer, making as many improvements as you can.

Good answer

Feature 1:
Model dwellings were new housing developments designed in the 1870s. The Peabody Estate consisted of new blocks containing nearly 300 flats.
Feature 2:
The Whitechapel Estate model dwellings were an example of the first slum clearance programme, conducted in the 1870s. The Estate was built where previously narrow courtyards filled with cramped and unhealthy houses had stood.

The answer has identified two features and describes them in more detail. The origin of the Estate is described very clearly. There is a description of what problems the new houses overcame.

Verdict

This is a good answer because it gives two clear features of 'Model' dwellings and gives extra detail to make the descriptions more precise.

Sources for use with Section A

Source A

From a report in the *East London Advertiser* newspaper, published 15 September 1888. The writer is commenting on Metropolitan Police Commissioner, Sir Charles Warren's decision to bring in soldiers to help police Whitechapel.

The double stupidity of weakening his detective force and strengthening his ordinary police force from reserves and the military destroys two safeguards of a community. It deprives it of a specially trained force of men with brainpower specially adapted for detective work and it takes away the old community constable, to be replaced by a man with a few years' military service, but with no other qualification for serving the public. Nothing has indeed been more characteristic of the hunt for the Whitechapel murderer than the lack of local knowledge displayed by the police. They seem to know little of the dark alleyways of the neighbourhood and still less of the bad characters who swarm through them.

Source B

A sketch for the *East London Observer*, 13 October 1888, on the training of bloodhounds.

248—Oct. 20, 1888—THE PENNY ILLUSTRATED PAPER—249

SIR CHARLES WARREN'S NEW CRIMINAL TRACKERS: MR. BROUGH'S BLOODHOUNDS BEING TRAINED.

Paper 1, Question 2a

Study Sources A and B in the Sources Booklet (see page 192).

How useful are Sources A and B for an enquiry into the methods used in the police hunt for the Whitechapel murderer in 1888?

Explain your answer, using Sources A and B and your own knowledge of the historical context. **(8 marks)**

Exam tip

Consider the strengths and weaknesses of the evidence. Your evaluation must link to the enquiry and use contextual knowledge. Your reasons (criteria) for judgement should be clear. Include points about:

- What information is relevant and what can you infer from the source?
- How does the provenance (nature, origin, purpose) of each source affect its usefulness?

Basic answer

Source A is useful because the 'East London Advertiser' tells us that Sir Charles Warren was stupid, because he took away from the murder inquiry the police with the best brainpower to solve it.

> Some useful information is taken from the source. The answer suggests an inference –'best brainpower to solve it', but does not really explain or develop this.

Source A is also useful because Warren was the Metropolitan Police Commissioner, although it is also not useful because this was from a local newspaper that wanted to sell lots of copies when unusual events were going on. The author is describing a couple of things that were wrong with the inquiry.

> Comments are made about the nature of the source, but they assume that a general need by newspapers to sell copies makes this unreliable. There is a need to include additional knowledge to evaluate the source.

Source B is useful because the sketch shows that the police were using new ideas such as tracker dogs to try to hunt down Jack the Ripper. It is reliable because we know that Sir Charles Warren ordered an experiment to see if bloodhounds could follow a scent.

> Comments show that there is information that can be taken from the sketch. Knowledge is added to show that the sketch is reliable, however the candidate doesn't mention that the bloodhounds were never used in the investigation. It begins to make an inference ('using new ideas…'). It would be stronger with more developed evaluation.

Verdict

This is a basic answer because:

- it has taken relevant information from both sources and shown some analysis by beginning to make an inference
- it has added in some relevant contextual knowledge and used it for some evaluation of one of the sources, but knowledge needs to be used for both
- it does not explain criteria for judgement clearly enough to be a strong answer. The evaluation using the provenance of the sources should be more developed.

Use the feedback to re-write this answer, making as many improvements as you can.

Paper 1, Question 2a

Study Sources A and B in the Sources Booklet (see page 192).

How useful are Sources A and B for an enquiry into the methods used in the police hunt for the Whitechapel murderer in 1888?

Explain your answer, using Sources A and B and your own knowledge of the historical context. **(8 marks)**

Exam tip

Consider the strengths and weaknesses of the evidence. Your evaluation must link to the enquiry and use contextual knowledge. Your reasons (criteria) for judgement should be clear. Include points about:

- What information is relevant and what can you infer from the source?
- How does the provenance (nature, origin, purpose) of each source affect its usefulness?

Good answer

Source A is an account by the 'East London Advertiser', written during the Whitechapel murders in 1888. We can see that the writer has identified particular weaknesses in the police inquiry, such as pulling out detectives ('with brainpower') and replacing useful local police with random army types ('with no other qualification'). Newspapers were often critical of the police and deliberately obstructed the police with fake letters, etc. It is accurate because Warren did take the steps described. But many sensible things had been introduced into the inquiry, including visits to several pawnbrokers' shops to try to track down missing rings from a victim. So Source A is a bit one-sided, ignoring good police work.

> Good analysis of the source linked to relevant knowledge. Own knowledge is used to support the comments on the provenance of this source. It is compared with other similar sources.

Source B is useful because it shows a method of investigating the Whitechapel murders. The portrayal is somewhat accurate because Warren ordered an experiment with bloodhounds in Hyde Park, but is unreliable because these tests never got beyond public parks and this sketch shows Whitechapel streets. As a local newspaper known for exaggeration, it is probably making gentle fun of the new police method ('Mr Warren's new criminal trackers'). Because of this limited purpose, it does not say anything about logical police methods, but does show clearly one reason why the police were criticised.

> Strengths and limitations of the source are shown and contextual knowledge is used in the evaluation, which also comments on the nature of the source, using details and taking examples from both the sketch and its caption.

Verdict

This is a good answer because:

- it has analysed both sources, making inferences from them
- it has used contextual knowledge in the evaluation of both sources
- the evaluation takes provenance into account and explains criteria clearly when making judgements.

Paper 1, Question 2b

Study Source A (see page 192).

How could you follow up Source A to find out more about the methods used in the police hunt for the Whitechapel murderer in 1888?

In your answer, you must give the question you would ask and the type of source you could use.

Complete the table below. **(4 marks)**

(see page 192)

Exam tip

Make sure your detail to follow up, your question and your suggested type of source all link and that you explain how the source could help answer the question.

Basic answer

Detail in Source A that I would follow up:

The local police were replaced by men with a few years' military service but no local experience.

Question I would ask:

How many local police officers were involved in the hunt for the Ripper?

> The question is linked to the detail to be followed up.

What type of source I could use:

Police station records.

How this might help answer my question:

They would include reports.

> The choice of source is unspecific and the explanation does not show how the source would help answer the question.

Verdict

This is a basic answer because the explanation of the choice of source is not developed. The candidate needs to be more specific about what type of police station records would be useful, and why.

Use the feedback to re-write this answer, making as many improvements as you can.

Paper 1, Question 2b

Study Source A (see page 192).

How could you follow up Source A to find out more about the methods used in the police hunt for the Whitechapel murderer in 1888?

In your answer, you must give the question you would ask and the type of source you could use.

Complete the table below. **(4 marks)**

(see page 192)

Exam tip

Make sure your detail to follow up, your question and your suggested type of source all link and that you explain how the source could help answer the question.

Good answer

Detail in Source A that I would follow up:

The local police were replaced by men with a few years' military service, but with no local experience.

Question I would ask:

How many of the men assigned to the Ripper investigation had strong knowledge of the local community?

The answer has given a question linked directly to the issue identified.

The type of source I could use:

Metropolitan Police records showing the reports of, and beats patrolled by, H Division officers, and the service history of the officers.

How might this help answer my question:

If most of the reports of daily activity, particularly beat reports, were from long-serving men in H Division this would show that the investigation was being carried out by men with local knowledge, but if many reports were from men recently recruited from the army, it would show up the weakness suggested in Source A.

The explanation is linked back to the question for follow-up and the type of source chosen.

Verdict

This is a good answer because connections between the source details, the question and the source chosen for follow-up are securely linked.

Answers to recap questions

Chapter 1

1. Nobles, freemen, serfs
2. Tithingmen
3. Two of: trial by boiling water, trial by hot iron, trial by cold water
4. Poaching
5. One of: blinding, castration, mutilation, hanging
6. Somebody who has run away to avoid being arrested or tried. There was no punishment for killing an outlaw.
7. Statute of Labourers
8. Treason
9. The Pope
10. Someone accused of a crime could claim protection in certain important churches – they could 'hide out' in the church; this was called 'sanctuary'.

Chapter 2

1. The criminal was hanged, taken down before they were dead, their stomach opened and, finally, the body was cut into four parts.
2. Make the treatment of vagrants more consistent from parish to parish
3. Patrol the street at night to catch criminals in the act
4. Bridewell
5. Pillory, stocks
6. 283
7. *Demonologie*
8. North America
9. 1605
10. Witchfinder General

Chapter 3

1. Administering an illegal oath
2. 1778
3. *The State of Prisons in England and Wales*
4. Newgate
5. A punishment in which prisoners walked on a revolving wheel
6. 1856
7. Henry Fielding
8. Home Secretary
9. London
10. Two of: Dick Turpin, Jack Shepherd, Black Harry

Chapter 4

1. Speeding, drink-driving
2. Verbal or physical abuse of somebody because of their race, gender, sexuality, or disability
3. 1991
4. Police Community Support Officer
5. Young offenders
6. Tribunals
7. 1993
8. Age at which someone can be prosecuted and punished for committing a crime
9. Limiting access to buildings and digital devices, for example, using body feature recognition
10. New Hall, Wakefield

Index

Acknowledgements

Text Credits:

BBC: Interpretation 1 from Inside The Medieval Mind, episode 2 transcribed, BBC/OU, with permission from the BBC. 22; **Bloomsbury Publishing**: Gaunt, R. A. Sir Robert Peel: The Life and Legacy (Vol. 2). © 2010, IB Tauris. Used with Permission 102; **Crown Copyright**: © Crown Copyright. Contains public sector information licensed under the Open Government Licence v3.0. 118; **History Press**: Adrian Gray, Crime and Criminals of Victorian London, © 2006, Phillimore. Used with Permission 152; **History Today Ltd**: Swinging Sixties: The Abolition of Capital Punishment by Liz Homans, December 12, 2008, Volume 58, © History Today Ltd. Used with Permission 122; **Liddle Collection**: Foister, J, Diary of Jack Foister, © 1916, Liddle Collection. Used with Permission 128; **Oxford University Press**: G.M. Young, Victorian England: portrait of an age, © 1936, Oxford University Press 4, 102; **Parliamentary Copyright**: Policing In The Metropolis, Mr. William Pitt (Croydon North-West), House of Commons Hansard, Volume 38, February 28, 1983, © Parliamentary Copyright. Contains Parliamentary information licensed under the Open Parliament Licence v3.0. 117; **Peace Pledge Union**: Joyce Allen, Peace Pledge Union (PPU). Used with Permission 129; **Spartacus Educational Publishers Ltd**: Number of people executed for heresy in England and Wales, © Spartacus Educational Publishers Ltd 43; **Telegraph Media Group Limited**: Philip Johnston, Duncan Gardham and Richard Edwards, MI5 trailed 7/7 bombers for a year, May 01, 2007, © Telegraph Media Group Limited. Used with Permission 111; **Vicky Pryce**: Prisonomics © Vicky Pryce 2013 reproduced by permission of Biteback Publishing 123.

Photo Credits:

(Key: b-bottom; c-centre; l-left; r-right; t-top)

AKG Images: AKG Images 27, Archie Miles/AKG Images Cover, 1; **Alamy Stock Photo**: Pictorial Press Ltd 91, 163, Chronicle 72, 85, 89, 93, 128, 173, John Frost Newspapers 175, British Library 162, Interfoto 24, Granger, NYC/Granger Historical Picture Archive 42, Mirrorpix/Trinity Mirror 110, Paul Doyle 109, The History Collection 97, The Picture Art Collection 10, 15, Album 159; **Crown Copyright**: © Crown Copyright. Contains public sector information licensed under the Open Government Licence v3.0. 60r, 60l, 100, 157, 151; **Getty Images**: Fotosearch/Archive Photos 45, 64, Roger Viollet Collection 4, 57, 54, Mary Evans Picture Library 94r, Hulton Archive 94l, 146, Photo12/UIG 76, 77, Maodesign 184, Corbis Historical 161, Guildhall Library & Art Gallery/Heritage Images 40, 55, 83, Evening Standard/Hulton Archive 122, Mike Moore/Hulton Archive 124, Popperfoto 131, 132, Universal History Archive/Universal Images Group 8, 35, 62, Maodesign/DigitalVision Vectors 181, Keystone-France/Gamma-Keystone 106, 114, Express Newspapers 177, Ann Ronan Pictures/Print Collector/Hulton Archieves 23, Monty Rakusen 115t, The Cartoon Collector/Print Collector 81, 82, Photo by DeAgostini 20, Tommaso Boddi 53, World History Archive 168; **Library of Congress**: Library of Congress Prints and Digital Photographs [LC-USZC4-10943] 127; **Mary Evans Picture Library**: Peter Higginbotham Collection 158, 160, 185, David Lewis Hodgson 174t; **Shutterstock**: Shutterstock 115b, London News Pictures 9, 116; **Solo Syndication**: Daily Sketch/Associated Newspapers Ltd 121; **The Bridgeman Art Library Ltd**: Bridgeman Images 17, 179l, British Library Board 25, Look and Learn/Peter Jackson Collection 153, 179r, 192, Peter Newark Historical Pictures 174b.